David Lean.

David Lean
An Intimate Portrait

Sandra Lean
with Barry Chattington

UNIVERSE

To David,

and one who gave us so much help,

hindrance and humour, Red – my Burmese cat.

First published in the United States of America in 2001
by UNIVERSE PUBLISHING

A Division of Rizzoli International Publications, Inc.
300 Park Avenue South
New York, NY 10010

Copyright©2001 Sandra Lean and Barry Chattington

2001 2002 2003 2004 2005 2006/ 10 9 8 7 6 5 4 3 2 1

Printed in Italy

Creative Consultant: Tim Garland-Jones
Original Picture Research and Art Direction: Michael Ross
Based on an original design by Michael Tighe

For André Deutsch:
Executive Editor: Sarah Larter
Art Director: Peter Bailey
Jacket Design: Alison Tutton
Production: Garry Lewis

THIS PAGE: A picture of David taken by his brother Edward in the 1930s.
PREVIOUS PAGES: David on the terrace on Narrow Street by Jill Pennington.

CONTENTS

INTRODUCTION

If I wanted to do an autobiography I would write it myself as a book
with a lot of photographs

DAVID LEAN

He is a dreamer and adventurer who says to us: see the world through my eyes.

GREGORY PECK: AMERICAN FILM INSTITUTE LIFE ACHIEVEMENT AWARD MARCH 8, 1990

The Bridge on the River Kwai, Lawrence of Arabia, Doctor Zhivago – these are just a few of David's films that have stood the test of time. As children or adults, male or female, we remember the courage, the romance and the emotions of the wonderful characters played by Julie Christie, Peter O'Toole, Alec Guinness and Omar Sharif. Through his films we have been carried on a magic carpet to corners of the world we might not otherwise have seen. But, if asked, do we all know who directed these masterpieces and can we put a face to him? I wonder if many could answer these questions.

David was, and still is, revered by his peers and it has been said by many of them that he was the ultimate film-maker. He was a "viceroy, a field marshal". He used vast canvases, thousands of extras and hundreds of technicians. Many dissertations and books have been written about his film-making, which was unique. All these words are eloquent and have been written by the dedicated for whom I have the utmost respect but, after reading almost everything that has been written about David, I found myself thinking that nothing exists tells me **who** he was and how he – a man who was described as a rather cold and unfeeling perfectionist – translated and transferred such extraordinary emotion on to celluloid. To most of the world he remains an enigma; only a handful of people were allowed into the intimacy of his life.

As David's sixth and last wife, he often said to me, "please, if anyone is going to write a book about me, I am concerned that it should contain plenty of illustrations. Really good pictures … that's all, just bloody good pictures … with pictures I feel as though I'm swimming in my own water."

After all, his films concentrate on images rather than dialogue as he said:

The moments you remember in movies are not often dialogue. They are images – pictures with music and sound that move you. It is emotions not spectacle that make a picture big and the most important thing of all is to find a story that you can fall in love with.

These words convinced me that a book containing the highly personal accounts of the people who came into contact with David, through his work and private life, should be written. I decided not to tackle his life chronologically, the elusive man can only be reached through the components that go into film-making. For David, personal life and work were inseparable. Instead the chapters follow the paradigm of a film budget from the initial treatment to the finished film with his personal story interweaving throughout. Thus the vertebrae of his life.

An incident last year further committed me to put pen to paper – or rather fingers to computer. David and my mother were both born on March 25. I walked to Brompton Oratory on that date to light a candle in memory of them and remained in the peaceful atmosphere listening to the choir. As I opened the door to leave and stood on the steps, an elderly lady, clearly disabled, approached me and touched my arm. She had been watching me for some time, she said and enquired if all was well with me. I thanked her for her kindness and replied that all was well and we continued talking.

I explained my mission. After a while she asked my name. When I told her, her face lit up "Lean, as in David Lean?" she asked. I nodded. Because of her disability she had never been able to travel and her parting words were, "I will never forget him. Because of his films he has enabled me to travel to countries I could not physically visit and to meet people I would not have otherwise known. I will be forever grateful to him."

Very little has been said about the man who sacrificed his personal life for that of his art, it was always subservient to making movies. Yet, without a strong understanding of human emotion how could a man create so many films that touched the hearts of millions?

Sandra Lean

OPPOSITE: **David in the doorway of the Moulin, our French home.**

FOREWORD BY OMAR SHARIF

Much has been written about David Lean, all of it quite fascinating. Understandably so, since we all agree he was probably one of the great film-makers of our time. However, what most people don't know is **who** David Lean was. I feel I know a lot about him, but only as much as he would allow any man to know – in two words, not much! I think he was more vulnerable and less protective of his personality in his relationships with women. This was perhaps as a result of his Quaker background or some special bond with his mother. I am only guessing. But if ever someone knew David, surely it was Sandra. Therefore, I think this book is essential to those of us, whether or not film-lovers, who want an insight into David Lean: the man, the husband, the lover and the Englishman with a left-hand Rolls. He was, as I knew him, a human being as Anglo-Saxon as they come and as romantically oriental as ever I have known.

I recall sitting next to the pilot of a small one-engine plane circling the Jordanian desert. In the middle of nowhere, a man – a lonely figure – was standing. He stepped towards me as I got off, surveying me from all angles with his piercing eyes. That was my first meeting with David. It changed my life. I think there and then he invented me. I let him do it because, somehow, I knew I was in good hands. I think he liked me for it. He liked only a few men, primarily Robert Bolt and, in a perverse way, Sam Spiegel. He loved some women, and most of all, perhaps because she was the last one, Sandra. She accompanied his last happy years when he put down his mask, as it were, and became the intimate person the whole world wanted to know. This book lifts the veil on the private David Lean.

OPPOSITE: **David and Omar during the filming of** *Lawrence of Arabia*.

1 TREATMENT

Big things have small beginnings.
LAWRENCE OF ARABIA

Births.
MARCH.

CROSSFIELD.—6th. At The Nook, Arnside, Sallie, wife of William Crossfield, junr., a daughter, who was named Winifred.

CLARK.—12th. At Hoshangabad, C. P., India, to G. E. and G. M. Clark, a daughter, who was named Elizabeth.

BAILEY.—18th. At 5, Kent House Road, Beckenham, Harriet Mary, wife of James Bailey, a daughter, who was named Rita Vera.

DOUGLAS.—21st. At 18, Wexford Street, Dublin, Emily, wife of John Douglas, a daughter, who was named Sarah Hilda.

LEAN.—25th. At 38, Blenheim Crescent, South Croydon, to Francis William Le Blount and Helena Annie Lean (*née* Tangye), a son, who was named David.

TAYLOR.—29th. At Malton, to Ernest E. and Katherine L. Taylor, a daughter, who was named Margaret Farrer.

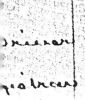

ABOVE: One of David's own early photographs of his brother Edward.

OPPOSITE PAGE, TOP: David's birth certificate; he was born on March 25, 1908. BOTTOM, CLOCKWISE FROM LEFT: David's mother, Helena Annie Lean; David as a young boy; his father, Francis William Le Blount Lean; and the newspaper announcement of David's birth.

IT IS NOT SURPRISING that David entered the creative world of movie-making as he always regarded his mother's side of the family as "quite artistic and an interesting lot." Yet he did not realize his own artistic qualities until he had completed the normal path of education. He is quoted as saying that his childhood was "a happy one", although later in life he admitted that, in fact, it was intolerable. He tried desperately to achieve what was expected of him and failed miserably. Perhaps David's father did not spend enough time talking to his young son to bring these hidden talents to the surface. David used to express this as "tickling a talent".

The family were strict Quakers and somewhat blinkered. Academia overruled any creative ability. While his brother, Edward, excelled academically, David remained a "dud" at school; his headmistress even wondered whether he would even be able to read or write. **"David daydreams,"** his reports revealed.

David admitted to being neither interested in mathematics nor good at it. I used to watch him counting on his fingers. Early days and school caused him to be insecure for the rest of his life and he felt inferior in the company of "highbrow" people.

In adolescence his life became even more difficult. He described his mother as a "sweet and very pretty woman" and from all accounts, he was her favoured son. However, when he was sixteen his father left her for another woman. According to David, she never recovered and I think the split and the ensuing divorce left a heavy cloud over him for the rest of his life. David found it difficult to handle his mother's emotions. "I felt very lonely and dreaded the thought of returning home in the evening so I sat in the refreshment bar at Victoria Station and took the last train to Croydon hoping that when I reached home my mother would be asleep." When he finally arrived, he was careful not to make a noise as he stepped on the gravel path leading up to the house. He would open the door, step cautiously into the hall and invariably hear his mother calling, "Is that you Dave?" His reply, "Who else do you think it could be?" When I think about it now of course he drew on his own experience in the refreshment bar at Victoria and used it in *Brief Encounter*.

His mother's constant weeping carried into David's own life and relationships; he could not abide to hear any woman he was with crying. I think it evoked earlier feelings that he had blocked from his memory, with which he simply could not cope.

When the going became rough and a relationship interfered with film-making, he simply cut that relationship from his life and never referred to it again. "You see you must cut. Anything that is finished is finished. You must just pretend people aren't there. Once you've made that decision, **you've just got to cut people out of your life."**

David craved the affection, sympathy and understanding that he did not receive in childhood. Only a woman who was "at one with herself"

OPPOSITE: David's brother, Edward Lean, at the BBC World Service in the 1940s.

LEFT AND BELOW: David's early influences: the Tangyes Engineering company, a children's comic, cinema and radio.

BOTTOM LEFT: David with director, Gabriel Pascal, on the set of *Major Barbara* (1941) on which David worked as editor.

LEFT: Leighton Park School where David spent his teenage schooldays.

RIGHT: Boot Parade.

BELOW LEFT: The formal school photograph.

The flip side of David's school life – photography, wireless and, ABOVE, the Central Cinema, Reading.

could stand up to his needs. He was possessive of the women in his life and I recall that he was at his happiest when I was at his side while he worked. Concentration was of immense importance to him as it was difficult for him to convey the images in his head into words. I learned not to interrupt him. He would ask my opinion from time to time but I never initiated a conversation. This would have sown the seeds of discontent in him.

Lonely, longing for the intelligence of his brother and lacking affection from his parents, David escaped into another world – that of his wireless. He became expert in taking it apart and reassembling it. Even then, he became fascinated with what went on "behind the scenes." This goes hand in hand with cutting a film and putting it together, which would eventually lead him to editing.

He was not allowed to go to the cinema but the family's "Mrs. Mop", a woman called Mrs Egerton, entertained him by running around the kitchen table and doing a Charlie Chaplin impersonation. David later came to admire Chaplin and his films, they touched him enormously. We watched them together when we lived in Narrow Street, Limehouse and I noticed tears running down his cheeks. He had told me about Mrs Egerton and I somehow thought that she had given him something denied to him by his parents in childhood. I'm sure that watching those films recalled those memories – another reason for the tears.

Amid the loneliness, he did have another great "friend" – the Box Brownie camera given to him by his Uncle Clement for his eleventh birthday. With this he proved finally to himself and the family that he could do something well. The camera accompanied him everywhere; even to school where he learned to develop his own photographs. He became aware of composition when he was taken on holiday to Switzerland, France and the Mediterranean. At last he was emerging from his shell and it was probably the camera that subconsciously laid the groundwork for his great escape from Croydon and the family.

Discovering the movies and photography, David knew which direction he wanted to follow. The drudgery of working in his father's accountancy firm checking and re-checking figures, which he did when he finished school, confirmed to him that this was something he was not going to do for the rest of his life and, via his Aunt Edith and his father, he got his first job as a tea boy at Gaumont-British Studios in Lime Grove. He was so excited by the atmosphere there that he would do anything connected with the movies.

The cinema was such magic to me. I didn't really believe movies were made in a studio, or that one could go into the so-called "business". I never thought I personally could go into that box of magic.

David's early loves –
Charlie Chaplin and
the Box Brownie camera.

He learned quickly and eventually landed in the cutting room. This is where he first learned the importance of editing and telling a story visually. He told me that he often sidled up to people when he came out of the theatre and heard them say "Oh, wasn't the photography wonderful!" but, as he commented, "Often they're not talking about the photography at all, rather they are referring to cutting."

In 1930 David married his first cousin, Isabel Lean, who had become pregnant after a romantic trip they had made to the Continent. Their son, Peter, was born later that year. By now, David was working hard and spent little time with the family. No money and a crying child caused the first big cut in his life. The marriage lasted just two years. In 1932, David walked out on Isabel and Peter. As well as becoming the most efficient editor in celluloid he had already become quite adept at it in his private life.

David was by now the highest paid "cutter" in England and very much sought after. He was also a very handsome, charismatic man.

David's progress in pictures went from *Boy's Own* (ABOVE) and watching *The Mark of Zorro* at the Orpheum to directing his first movie with Noël Coward.

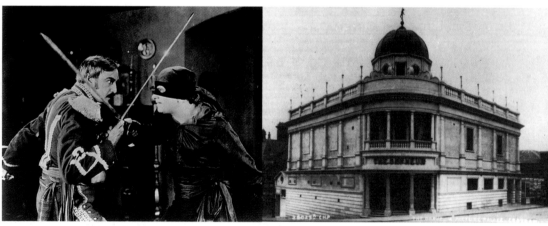

He could have had any woman he wanted. He fell in love with Kay Walsh, an actress, who became his second wife in 1940.

His first credit for directing was in 1942, alongside Noël Coward on *In Which We Serve*. David was originally to be the director's assistant but he insisted on being credited co-director.

"Whoever has heard of you?" asked Noël. **"They soon will,"** said David and he was hired for the job. Eventually, Noël became bored with directing and, as he was in the film himself, his concentration veered towards the acting. One day he said to David "My dear, I'll leave it all to you." David's debut as sole director came with Noël's *This Happy Breed* (1944) with Anthony Havelock-Allan as producer and Ronald Neame as cameraman. Together, the three formed Cineguild, which produced seven of David's films.

OPPOSITE: *The Hound of the Baskervilles* (1921) was David's first taste of the cinema. It was directed by Maurice Elvey, with whom he later worked.

AMUSEMENTS

From FRIDAY, Nov. 29th, 1918

CROYDON

To SUNDAY, Dec. 8th, 1918

THEATRE

GRAND
High Street
(Ring up : 12)

CINEMAS

HIPPODROME
Crown Hill
(Ring up : 1444)

ORPHEUM
Scarbrook Hill
(Ring up : 1827)

PALACE
Thornton Heath
(Ring up : 1052)

PALLADIUM
North End
(Ring up : 1155)

PICTURE
HOUSE, North End
(Ring up : 203)

SCALA
North End
(Ring up : 1620)

SAT. & SUN.

WEEK-END
Cinema, Surrey St.
(Ring up : 1719)

RAY
In THE
HIRED MAN

MACISTE,
The Strong
Man

MY 4 YEARS
IN GERMANY
By Amb. Jas. W. Gerard
IN ITS ENTIRETY

NOV. 30 & DEC. 1

SOWING
THE WIND
Featuring
TOM MOORE

ILENT MAN ; &
lder Arms
ARLIE CHAPLIN

MILES
ER
In BEAUTY
THE ROGUE

REEDOM
WORLD
With
K. LINCOLN

till 10.30

The Only
AY
URES
In Croydon

ABOVE AND RIGHT: Noël Coward gave David his first directorial break on *In Which We Serve*.

ABOVE: Director Bernard Vorhaus took David out of Movietonews to edit *Money For Speed* (1933) (LEFT) a great progress from working on *Quinneys* an early job at Gaumont (RIGHT).

To me, this chapter in David's life is rather like looking at him through a camera lens. The beginning, Croydon, a "close-up"; the lens gets wider as he "stretches his eye." The world is his oyster. However, he's not there yet. The climb will be tough; he is nervous and apprehensive but, at the same time, he is determined and passionate. He expected high standards from actors only because he had set himself even higher standards. He was on his own now – the loner just like the characters in his films, the single person set against grand undertakings. His movies reflected his own life, the single brooding perfectionist force behind great endeavours. Thereafter, bigger lenses, bigger budgets, far away locations, epic films, more women and more cuts.

It's that way with every Englishman. Lawrence was to young English boys the last word in exotic heroes. We saw pictures of him in that exotic dress and headgear. We heard Lowell Thomas sing his praises over the radio. But then Lawrence is an enigma and I've always been fond of enigmas. I like the "flawed heroes". Perfection is dull. When I was a boy, I would pick on the most eccentric person in the room and study him.

DAVID LEAN, WORLD PREMIERE OF THE RESTORED
LAWRENCE OF ARABIA, NEW YORK, 1989

LEFT AND BELOW:
David's fellow cutters
Merrill White and Dickie
Best and one of the
original Moviolas (the
cutting machine used by
David early in his career).

BELOW: A poster for Cineguild.

OPPOSITE: David at the
beginning of his directorial career.

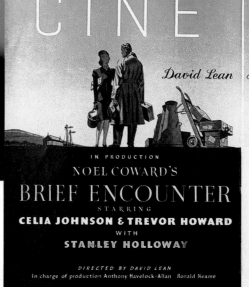

Authors of
excellence.

Joseph Conrad.　　　H. G. Wells.　　　Boris Pasternak.　　　Terence Rattigan.

ABOVE: Planners of dreams,
David and Robert Bolt.

M. Forster.　　Charles Dickens.　　H. E. Bates.　　Pierre Boulle.　　T.E. Lawrence.

2 STORY AND SCENARIO

The most important thing of all is to find a script you can fall in love with.

DAVID LEAN

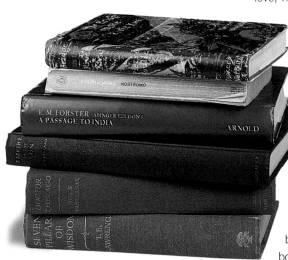

THE TWO LOVERS sat in the window, oblivious to any distraction. Behind them the Thames flowed lazily by. There were long pauses in their conversation, then, like a tennis match, a quick-fire, back-and-forth volley as they exchanged words and solutions. They had fallen in love, not with each other, but with a new venture. There was a new script to be written, a new film to be made. This scene had been enacted many times before, starting in the Jordanian desert in the 1960s and then through various countries and situations around the world.

These two men had found a story they could cherish and were now preparing it for a movie that would be filmed in South America and France. In David's study in Narrow Street, London, they were honing the images and words that would excite a worldwide audience about the lives of men who were gripped by the love of silver. Ironically, the story in Joseph Conrad's *Nostromo* ran parallel to both their lives: in the book the characters were obsessed by the production of a precious metal, whereas these two senior figures of the film business were refining a path to condense a six-hundred page book into a two-hour movie. And they were in love with their task.

It was fascinating to witness Robert Bolt and David working with each other. One overweight and struggling with the frustration of dysphasia caused by his stroke, the other needing a clear vision to encapsulate the thoughts of a character in, at most, a look.

"Why do you think he does that in the book?" David would muse. Robert would think, then with a mighty effort, struggle to be able to give the insight needed for the action. Often the answer was sprinkled with many "fuck its" as he endeavoured to find the words that were in his head but were being prevented from smooth delivery by the cruel insult to his brain.

Once the answer had been articulated: "Well done, Robert."

Smiles from them both, then Robert would fling his arms wide with his hands emphasizing the gesture and **"LOVVERRLY"** would ring out.

It was a relationship that had begun nearly thirty years before on *Lawrence of Arabia*.

David and Sam Spiegel, his producer on *The Bridge on the River Kwai* (1957), were equally enthusiastic about making T. E. Lawrence the subject of their next film and by the spring of 1961 preparations were well in hand. David was dissatisfied with the script but, under pressure to begin filming as soon as possible, he and art director, John Box, started to look for locations in Jordan. Meanwhile, Sam set up a meeting in London with Robert Bolt whose play *A Man for All Seasons*, about Sir Thomas More, had recently opened to rave reviews. He persuaded Robert to join David in the desert.

The fact that Robert had spent time with Sam worried David, making

their first meeting unsuccessful. The icy greeting in the desert between director and new writer was also due to the driven director's suspicion of intellectuals. Christopher Hampton, who collaborated with David on the script of *Nostromo*, probably best expresses this attitude: "David detested intellectuals as a breed; he thought them snobbish, condescending, dishonest and impotent."

However, David's respect for Robert grew as the writer took to adapting Lawrence's *The Seven Pillars of Wisdom*. Robert was also captivated by images and enjoyed the challenge of seeing how the words of the book could be replaced by pictures. This partnership bonded as they tried to find the best device to take the audience into the desert.

The conversation between the precise director and the word man can easily be envisaged:

"How do we get them from the comfortable staff offices in Cairo to the hottest place on the planet?"

Pause.

"With a match!"

"Huurray, very good, Robert," said David after folding his arms and pausing for a long time.

After the success of *Lawrence of Arabia* (1962) "the two" tackled Pasternak's *Doctor Zhivago* (1965). Robert said, "I've never done anything so difficult, that bugger Pasternak! It's like straightening cobwebs."

While researching this book, we discovered a four-page critique by Robert tucked inside David's copy of *Doctor Zhivago*. It is fascinating to

BELOW AND OPPOSITE: **David with Robert in presentation, production (with Sarah Miles), recreation, contemplation and realization.**

1. The essence of the book is in its style — a style of leisure. Contrary to most books & almost all films the style is the accidental. It is a poem. The film too must be a poem. This is a long book & a complex story. It will in any case have to be grossly simplified to get it into (say) 2½ hours. But if we merely simplify to that end, to get it into 2½ hours, we shall have merely an ordinary "fast-moving" story, an ordinary film. We must further simplify so that the story we are left with can be told in 2½ hours at leisure. Only then can we be true in our film to the essence of the book.

2. An adventure of the mind & heart, not of the body: Dr Z is almost always physically passive. If he were also mentally & spiritually passive there would be no story, but in fact he is the most active mind & spirit possible: a poet. This is our story & "action" (meaning physical action) must be subservient to this (as, but moreso, in the first half of LAWRENCE). An adventure of the mind & spirit is equivocal, shifting, does not proceed: "Because this, therefore that", is arbitrary, not logical. We must must Pasternak and our own understanding; we mustn't be frightened into "finding" a logical, physical, "because this, therefore that" story-line. Without being perversely obscure, we must follow a poetic, atmospheric, not a logical, continuity, climax & denouement.

3. But contrariwise NB how important to Dr Z's inner

life is the background of the Revolution & how violently Pasternak contrasts it - its harshness, its hard, sharp outlines, its ruthless action — to the gentle contemplating inner life of Dr Z. But it is background only; it sees it, is acted upon by it; takes almost no part in it. It is like a cataclysm of Nature as described by Pasternak, not an act of Man. This distinction, this contrast, between the violent events & his experience of them & what his inner life makes of them, is the whole point & we must preserve it. He must not, can not, be the "hero" of the action. He must be the "hero" of the film. Therefore it is not a film of action. The action is its background & must be conceived & shot so as to make that point. The background (physical) action must not outweigh the foreground (spiritual) story. En tin it is a quiet, thoughtful, book, though quietly thinking about violent things. Ergo a quiet, thoughtful, film.

4. We will be helped in the above (a) by the number of good intimate & internal scenes, (b) by the great importance attached by Pasternak to Nature & Natural beauty. But we must show this, not in epic eyefulls, flat on, but as seen through the eyes & mind of a deliberately thoughtful & contemplative man, a poet; filtered.

5. All this means that the film must be rhythmic— must move forwards by mood, state-of-mind, image, rhythmically controlled, not by "plot-development". As with the book so with the film, its style must be its content & vice versa. Its style must not be mer decoration of the content. Indeed, see page 256.

6. Pasternak is dangerously modest about Dr Z may have to take it upon ourselves to be a shade less factually we may have to make his status as
EG

ABOVE AND OPPOSITE:
Robert Bolt's original
notes for *Doctor Zhivago*.

writer + poet more clear early in the story. Psychologically we may have to emphasize more than Pasternak does the gentleness + humanity of his passive tolerance. But it's a fine shade - he mustn't become any kind of Saint. He is remarkable for the fineness of his perceptions, not for his moral intensity. And NB Pasternak makes him capable here + there of very crisp judgments + decision. He is not at all watery.

7. Music. It must be sparing, modest, mostly solo, duet, trio, an octet (say) for climaxes. Not an orchestra. It's an intimate ~~story~~ against an epic background. The music must strengthen the story, must not side with the background.

8. The casting! My god the difficulties! Zhivago + the two women (particularly Lara) have got to have moral dignity - without posturing or pomposity. Where on earth do we find this?

7. Cutting. Ought to be very bold. Not just "striking" but really authoritative, not "explaining" itself, but having the logic of our truth-telling. Pasternak himself does this. Again, it means we must know the truth we are telling - (not "know", but sense). This brings me back to point 1 which I am more + more sure of: We have to start with a really simple, fine shape - I mean narrative + then select our incidents to embody it, not as in LAWRENCE, select incidents + by ingenuity compel them to follow a narrative shape or line. If David will wear it, I'd like to use a deliberately clumsy, primitive or naive, not ingenious sort of cutting, the sort of cutting which is the film equivalent of: "once upon a time", and "five years passed". If we want to tell the audience that it's 1905 I'd like to ~~put~~ put the figure on the screen + proceed with our story, not "neatly" dovetail the information into the dialogue. Not kid the audience along, but offer them the story to consider.

8. How marvellously unsentimental Pasternak is. What unexpected things his people say, like living people, not like "characters".

9. To conclude: as a story it's second-rate; it's melodramatic, full of "co-incidences", pointless. But in the manner of the telling, the odd incidents, it is superb. The manner + the incidents, these are what must make the film good.

10. We are going to have to be delicate. Therefore it is at some point going to seem to us that we are being merely faint. We shall need the courage of our convictions if we are not to betray ourselves out of fright. But if we think it through first + in execution are precise, accurate, not clumsy or violent, we shall be OK.

11. The love story should be - must be - heartbreaking. I'm not sure Pasternak has done enough for us here. We may have to improve on him! But we must take great care of this, great care; he knows what he's about + it we try to be more overt than he is we may bring it all crashing to the ground. The whole thing is airborne, not built.

As from July 9th - Home Farm House,
Pylewell,
Lymington,
Hampshire.

see how closely the first notes of the screenplay mirrored the final production. One of Robert's notes says,

> To conclude – as a story it's second rate; it's melodramatic, full of "coincidences", pointless. But in the *manner of the telling*, the odd incidents, it is superb. The manner & the incidents, these are what must make the film good.

Beyond this conclusion the music, the casting and the cutting are discussed in the critique and written into the final script, showing how heavily the film-maker had influenced Robert.

The collaboration continued with *Ryan's Daughter* (1970), which is based on Gustave Flaubert's *Madame Bovary*. To give the story more life David gave Robert a detailed account of his ideas and they worked together through a long hot summer and produced the final screenplay.

This wonderful partnership created three of the cinema's best movies but it came to a premature end in Tahiti when David and Robert were working on a project based on the mutiny on the *Bounty*. At one point David was going to direct two major productions based on the story of Captain Bligh and Fletcher Christian. For many reasons, including scurrilous gossip about David, the critics' attack on *Ryan's Daughter* and Robert's unfortunate illness, the films were never made.

Robert and David split in 1979. They had been working in Tahiti for many months and although the work was going well there was a strain developing in their personal relationship. David loved the vast skies and sheer beauty of the South Seas. He was there with Sandy Hotz (who became his fifth wife many years later) living an orderly life. In contrast, Robert had separated from his wife, Sarah Miles, and was savouring all the delights these islands could offer. The immaculately dressed and meticulous David worried about Robert, who was not looking after himself and becoming dishevelled and overweight. Robert's way of life culminated in a heart attack in Los Angeles, after which he suffered a debilitating stroke. Although David rushed to help, certain people believed that his thrust for perfection in his work had caused the crisis. David was

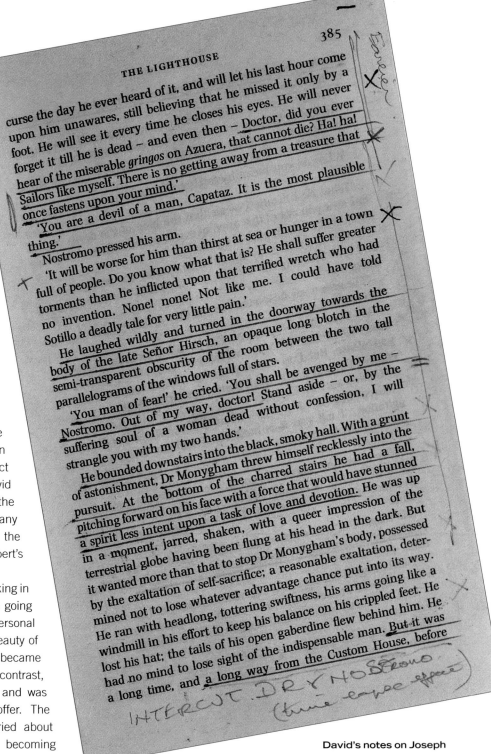

David's notes on Joseph Conrad's *Nostromo*.

LEFT: Madeleine Smith and the arsenic: her sensational Victorian murder trial was the basis of *Madeleine* (1950).

prevented from seeing Robert in hospital. They were not to meet again for fourteen years. Robert's own verdict on their working and personal relationship is eloquent: "When I'm working with David, it's hard for me to tell 'best' from 'most enjoyable'. **He is the most moving and endearing friend."**

Why didn't David take credit for his writing? Possibly because he did not think of himself as capable. For a man who is constantly quoted as saying "I'm not a word man," he wrote very well. It was only later when he gained more confidence in himself that he accepted credit where credit was due for the script of *A Passage to India* (1984). He took no credit on his earlier scripts and yet, in collaboration with the Cineguild team, Ronald Neame and Anthony Havelock-Allan, he adapted two novels by Charles Dickens, *Great Expectations* and *Oliver Twist* and four Noël Coward scripts, including *Brief Encounter*. He also worked with Norman Spencer and Wynyard Browne on the screen version of the stage play *Hobson's Choice*.

All but one of David's films were adapted from other works, although two were so far removed from their sources that they qualified for original screenplays. Ironically, they both caused David a considerable amount of anguish. He directed *Madeleine* (1950), based on a real-life Victorian murder scandal, at the request of his third wife, Ann Todd, who wanted to play the starring role. It was David's least favourite film and his last with Cineguild. And *Ryan's Daughter* was so badly mauled by the critics that David did not make another film for years afterwards.

The only Lean film with a truly original screenplay was *The Sound Barrier*, shot in the summer of 1951. The story was based on David's own research into the British aircraft industry, which also led to his enduring love for Rolls-Royce engines. Fine engineering held a fascination for him that probably came from his mother's family who were Cornish inventors. "I'd always wanted to make an adventure film about man's exploration into the unknown," David told the *New York Times*. "Now here was this 'Sound Barrier'– invisible, yet able to tear an aeroplane to pieces. Man's assault on this treacherous mass of air seemed to me the great modern adventure story."

David's enthusiasm sold the idea to Alexander Korda but he still needed to turn his research into a screenplay and for this he approached Terence Rattigan with whom he had worked when he edited *French without Tears* (1939). David had taken a year to research the idea, and gave Rattigan a notebook containing three hundred closely written pages. But it was not until Korda and David took the writer to watch a jet fly low at Farnborough, and he was introduced to the test pilots – "quiet young men, absolutely unlike the types I had known during the war" – that he agreed to write the script. Rattigan drew on his father to help him create the film's central character, Sir John Ridgeway, the pioneering aircraft builder who achieves his ambition, but only at the cost of his son's life. This character obviously interested David – he was domineering, frightened of being alone, craving human affection yet unable to show his true feelings. Another flawed hero.

It was the enigmatic character at the centre of *The Bridge on the River Kwai* that drew David to the story by Pierre Boulle, who was subsequently awarded the Academy Award for best screenplay, despite not having written a word of the script. This deception was necessary because of the McCarthy blacklisting of the writer who worked with David to create the screenplay. In fact, two blacklisted writers were involved in the venture, Carl Foreman and Michael Wilson. Carl wrote the first script, which David rejected. He then set to work with Michael Wilson to create the beautifully written final screenplay. Nevertheless, the secret had to be kept; otherwise "politics" would have prevented the film from receiving any awards. When *Kwai* was nominated for eight Academy Awards, David wrote to Michael:

Sam was in a fine old state because he was worried your wicked name might get out of the bag and "ruin our chances, baby". He told me that you were the one who was most anxious to have it hidden as it would put you out of work. Have no idea if this is true. Consequently, I lied like a trooper

LEFT: David with test pilot John Derry on the set of *The Sound Barrier* (1952).

ABOVE: David watching rehearsals.

BELOW: The British poster for *The Sound Barrier*.

RIGHT: David had a
continuing fascination
with Rolls Royce. This is
his own photograph.

BELOW: Queues for
The Sound Barrier.

to all who asked me if you did in fact write it. I made up a long story about Boulle and me in Paris – to overcome the people who said they just could not believe that a Frenchman who had never written a script in his life could produce such a work. It came to a climax when the Boston critics flew down here for a premiere and Sam had to tell them in my presence that I had done it with Boulle and didn't wish for a credit as directors and producers took it as part of their jobs.

As the suspicion over the identity of the true scriptwriter dragged on, Foreman kept the controversy alight until David met him one day at one of Sam's parties where he told him, "Carl, the next time that you claim that you wrote the script, I'll show them what you wrote." In fact David was bluffing as he hadn't got a copy of Carl's script but this ruse did quieten Foreman. David always wanted Michael's name on the credits and before he died he insisted I should make sure this happened. When *Kwai* was restored I made certain the name Michael Wilson appeared for screen-writing.

The selection of a story was of paramount importance to David who would spend many months or even years finding the right platform for his talent. The common feature in the majority of David's movies is that the lead parts reflected aspects of his own character or feelings. **They were about people he could understand.**

His desk always had a dictionary at one end and a thesaurus at the other; David was a legendary bad speller and never mastered the typewriter beyond a slow two-finger speed. He said this was an advantage as each word was painfully considered and therefore had to have a strong reason for use. Yet the long letters, including many to lovers, he wrote during his life proved he relished the written word and his prowess in words. His obsession with creating the right script probably originated from the belief that he was a "second-rate person." He felt from a very early age he was in the shadows of virtually everyone. Yet it is possible that this disdain spurred David to create a complex framework of pictures that told stories and delivered emotion to his audience.

David spent an enormous amount of time perfecting his scripts; he felt he could never work in the same way as Mike Curtiz, *Casablanca*'s director, who could have a script on Saturday and be shooting on Monday. He had to know and feel the characters, the rooms they were in and the reason they were there. To David, a film was shorthand, condensing a huge amount of information and feeling into sparse dialogue and magnificent pictures. The writing process allowed these thoughts to crystallize. Neil Jordan, who directed *Mona Lisa* and *The Crying Game*, articulated the importance of this stage for directors when he said:

As a director for hire you may as well be a traffic cop – not a very elevated place to be. You are just moving the furniture around, placing

the camera … when you write the script it is about how the images come to you and it's about how the film comes to you. If it comes from the writing it stays with you, it is more of an integral piece of work.

Possibly the knowledge gained when David worked as an editor of newsreels lasted all through his life, especially when he was working on a script. It is significant that Richard Attenborough called David "the great director of narrative." He would go over a book and meticulously underline the parts he thought were pivotal points or the drive of the work. It was these selected "highlights" that became the script; these incidents were the most memorable and gave the thrust to the story line. From these selections the script slowly grew with the overwhelming need for "continual flow", something that was reflected in his private life. "Babe, why can't you go in a straight line?" he would say to me, "do you have to do six things at the same time?"

David's ferocious concentration and fastidiousness in the search for perfection in every detail were legendary. For co-writers his methods appeared to be a perverse form of attrition as, just as they thought they were coming to the end of a script, there would be a long David Lean pause and he would announce, **"Now let's go back to the beginning."**

ABOVE: **Early days with the "Master" – Noël Coward on the set of *In Which We Serve*.**

OPPOSITE: **Later days – as the "Master".**

3 PRODUCTION UNIT

Producers look after money and opportunity
– directors look after passion and pictures.

FRANK O'CONNOR

DAVID WAS SUSPICIOUS of all producers. Why? Betrayal was the word that echoed in his head. He was loyal and expected loyalty in return. Instead, he had experienced deception from a number of producers – or "money men" as he referred to them.

This is perhaps strange because earlier in his career he worked with producers who had been extremely supportive. It wasn't as if he knew nothing about production on films as he himself had been a producer on his earlier films with Cineguild and had taken sole credit as producer on *The Sound Barrier*.

I do not want to weigh this book down with the technicalities of the film industry but as people outside the business often do not understand the different responsibilities in the roles of those at the head of the credits, I thought a little explanation and background would help explain why and how David's suspicion grew.

In the course of his career the role of the producer changed quite dramatically. In the early days, when David worked with Anthony Havelock-Allan, a producer's duties and responsibilities were to help the production run smoothly, enabling the director to concentrate on the images that appeared on the screen.

LEFT: **David with Sam Spiegel.**

ABOVE: Dino de Laurentiis says "H & G" (Hi and goodbye).

RIGHT: With charismatic Alexander Korda.

From the 1950s onward a producer's sole interest was in the financial aspect of the film, finding the "backers". Of David's films, *In Which We Serve* in 1942 through to *Madeleine* in 1950 were primarily financed by J. Arthur Rank, who allowed the creative team to run the productions. A highly successful businessman, Rank was a devout Methodist who believed the cinema could be used to show the Christian way of life while stemming the dominance of American influence on British cinemagoers. David edited Rank's first feature film *Turn of the Tide* in 1935. Although the picture was good, those who then controlled the British film industry shunned it. Rank or, as David and the rest of the film industry called him, "Uncle Arthur", used his money to buy many parts of the British film industry.

Rank and David had a number of similarities: they were both modest, both their fathers had forbade them to go to the cinema and thought they were "duds". David was asked his opinion of Rank in the late 1940s and wrote: "J. Arthur Rank is often spoken of as an all-embracing monopolist who must be watched lest he crush the creative talents of the British film industry. Let the facts speak for themselves … I doubt if any other group of film-makers anywhere in the world can claim as much freedom."

Unfortunately, by 1950 the accountants had taken the driving seat in the Rank Organisation. This, and a falling out with the other partners at Cineguild, forced David into the warm embrace of the mid-European film enthusiasts Alexander Korda, Ilya Lopert and Sam Spiegel for the next fourteen years. While these producers shared his passion for film-making, they were all by degrees much more dexterous than he was with money. Tony Reeves, David's lawyer since the 1980s, tells the following story, which illustrates David's financial grasp:

Occasionally David would express concern about his living expenses, he was worried that he could not afford to live in the manner he enjoyed. It wasn't just concern but a deep-seated paranoia. No matter how good his imagination for filling a 70mm screen – he could never understand the financial picture, even with the aid of graphs, charts and calculations, until one day I discovered the hidden talents and uses of sugar lumps.

We were having afternoon tea in his suite at the Dolde Grande Hotel in Zürich, I had been trying to explain that any worries he had were unfounded; the royalties from previous pictures were much higher than he was spending each year. He could not understand the position. So I emptied the sugar lumps on to the glass table and, using each sugar lump to represent £100,000, laid out a series of columns of ten to represent each million pound of assets and then new columns of sugar lumps, again each representing £100,000, to represent the interest and dividends which the investment columns of sugar lumps were producing. Then another column of sugar lumps of the same value were laid out to represent the average annual royalty he was receiving from all his previous films. I then asked David to work through with me his annual living expenses by units of £100,000. Not many sugar lumps were needed. Those "spend" sugar lumps were removed from the pile of annual receipts, leaving a significant number of surplus sugar lumps which were then added to the previous piles. David was then convinced that he could afford to maintain his lifestyle.

One producer David enjoyed working with was Alexander Korda, a Hungarian who, in the 1930s, had charmed an insurance company to support his ambition of creating major movies in Britain. Korda shared David's enthusiasm; he had a great respect for films and was passionate about them. He encouraged the making of *The Sound Barrier*, then *Hobson's Choice* (1954) and, with his New York partner Ilya Lopert, sent David to Venice to make *Summer Madness* (1955).

CLOCKWISE FROM TOP: John Brabourne (with David), Richard Goodwin "Partner Producers" on *A Passage to India*; Anthony Havelock-Allan – a lifetime friend on and off the set; Ilya Lopert; and "Uncle Arthur".

It was there that the role of producer and the power of money started to become more significant. Lopert used all the tricks at a producer's disposal to curb a director's inspiration. He employed an assistant director to time how long David took on shots. He ripped down the major set before David had really finished and before any reports of the rushes had come back to confirm the processed film was satisfactory. In fact, Lopert resorted to sending the main cameras back to Rome, leaving David with just a 16mm-Arriflex for the last week of filming. Finally, he had David thrown out of Italy; he had obviously bribed the Italian authorities to say the work permit had run out.

Even with these difficulties the picture was successful. Just before David left to pick up his New York Critics' Award for Best Director of the Year for *Summer Madness* (called *Summertime* in the U.S.) he met Sam Spiegel. Originally from Poland, Sam had produced the Oscar-winning *African Queen* and *On the Waterfront*. David's suspicion of anything he termed "grand" should have been alerted when, at that first meeting, Sam forced an oversized cigar on him. At the time David had been cleaned out financially by his divorce from Ann Todd and could not afford to have his teeth fixed, which may have clouded his judgement about the man who was to contribute so much to his mistrust of the "money men".

In size, shape, attitude and temperament, Sam Spiegel was almost a caricature of what filmgoers would expect of a typical film producer: he was mid-European, not tall but with a stomach that made up for his lack of height. Beneath this large girth were two very spindly legs. He liked his comforts, could be enormously charismatic and totally ruthless. All these attributes were brought into focus in Ceylon during the shooting of *The Bridge on the River Kwai*. The film industry abounds with "Sam" stories but I feel that this one, often told by David, encapsulates the "dealings" of this producer.

Sam rarely visited the location during shooting. However, on one of these rare visits, David wanted to share with his producer the harshness of the area so, with art director Don Ashton, David and Sam set off for the *Kwai* location.

As they drove to the site, with Sam wearing a shirt, shorts and beach shoes, David said,

"You need boots, Sam."

"Why?"

"There are blood-sucking leeches that live in the grass that we are going to walk through."

Sam was horrified that there were other creatures that had mastered the art of blood removal without recourse to lawyers. His eyes fell upon Don's boots.

"Take them off and give them to me."

Don dutifully unlaced his prized leathers, gave them to Sam and,

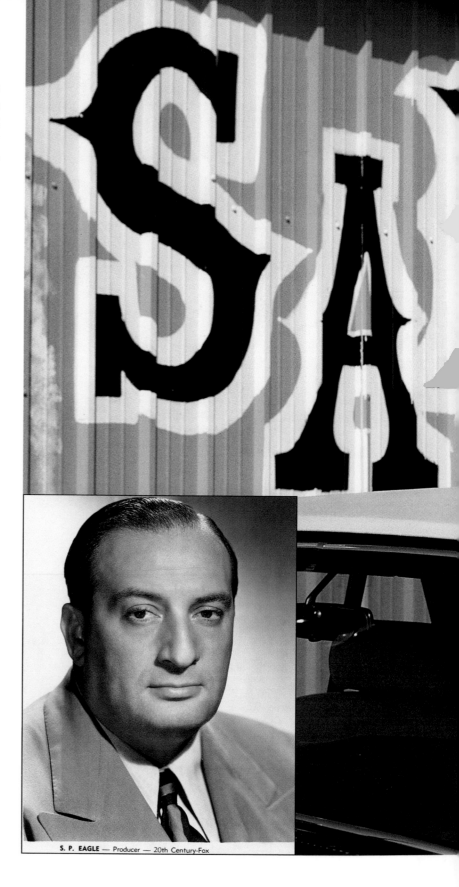

S. P. EAGLE — Producer — 20th Century-Fox

Occasionally David
saw the funny side
of his relationship
with Sam.

didn't know whether Sam loved or hated the footage. Finally he sent a telegram. Sam's reply read: "Baby, the quantity was so huge and the quality so poor, I didn't have the heart to tell you."

David suspected the reason behind this reply was that Sam wanted him to think that the film was not going to be successful and, moreover, that it would not generate much profit. In other words, what Sam really meant was: "Baby, don't expect much money out of this."

Both *Kwai* and *Lawrence* ran away with a clutch Academy Awards – seven each – including Best Picture for their producer, and of course Best Director for David. Sam still craved even more credit, petulantly trying to prove he was the reason these productions won their accolades. David even believed that some of the bad reviews for *Zhivago* could have been due to Sam.

In 1965 Sam was making *The Chase* with Arthur Penn while Carlo Ponti was producing *Doctor Zhivago* with David. *The Chase* had a dozen top stars headed by Marlon Brando, Jane Fonda and Robert Redford. It was billed as "a breathless explosive story of today". However, the film suffered from a literary format and attempted to pack too many characters and too many strong dramatic incidents into the two-hour running time. Perhaps Sam knew he had a turkey on his hands as he started to belittle David's efforts to the critics in a bid to undermine *Zhivago*. **"What a sod that man has turned out to be,"** wrote David,

… Sam had met with the critics a couple of weeks before and done a sort of benevolent uncle act about me. Words to the effect that I am great at detail but fail therefore in taking proper perspective of the whole. Then all about how he didn't send the rushes on *Kwai* and *Lawrence* but stayed in London "studying" them.

In spite of the old film adage "beware of the man who is whispering in your ear as he may be pissing in your pocket," some of the critics seem to have taken the bait. Judith Crist of the *Herald-Tribune*, after dismissing *Zhivago* as a "tedious epic-type soap opera" went on to infuriate David even more by implying that Sam Spiegel was responsible for earlier successes:

David Lean is one of those rare directors who has proved himself not once but twice master of the spectacular, with *The Bridge on the River Kwai* and *Lawrence of Arabia* (both, it is worth noting, with Sam Spiegel as producer; Carlo Ponti, a maker of spectaculars of a rather different batting average, produced *Doctor Zhivago*).

To counteract the critics, Bob O'Brien, in charge of MGM, spent an extra $1 million dollars on *Zhivago* publicity. The picture was a huge

now having no protection himself, drove off, leaving David and Sam to explore the jungle.

Sam wasn't an outdoor man and he bored easily. The heat and humidity soon exhausted him and he longed to get back to the air-conditioned hotel suite, so the recce was short-lived.

Back in the car David lit a cigarette and started investigating the top of his boots.

"What are you doing fiddling with your boots and that cigarette? You'll burn yourself," Sam asked irritably.

"What do you mean, what am I doing? I'm burning off the leeches from the top of my boots." Turning to Sam, David added quietly, "You ought to do the same, you know."

Sam looked down and, as he caught sight of a huge blood-filled leech at the top of his boot, a look of horror came over his face. "Stop the car, stop the car!" bellowed the scourge of the studio front office. The car screeched to a halt. David hit the jungle leech with his cigarette's glowing end and throw the blood-fattened creature out of the vehicle. Sam leapt out and stood staring at the squirming leech. After a moment, Sam's leather-clad foot stamped on the leech as he repeatedly jumped up and down shouting, "You have my blood, you have my blood, you have my blood."

Sam and David were supposed to be equal partners in their productions but many years after *Lawrence* David had still only received his shooting fee. This saddened him. He liked Sam; he admired his love and knowledge of movies, his risk-taking and the verve he brought to the production. Unfortunately, Sam wanted complete control. When David was in the Jordanian desert shooting *Lawrence* he had not heard anything from his producer for weeks. He

ABOVE: *Doctor Zhivago*'s producer, Carlo Ponti, wanted to cast his wife Sophia Loren as Lara. However, David insisted that the virginal looks of Julie Christie (OPPOSITE) prevailed.

LEFT: David with Rod Steiger and Bob O'Brien of MGM.

Production Unit 41

Yes ...

David and Sam through the years.

Yes ...

Yes ...

financial success and made more money for David than all his other productions put together. So some producers, Carlo Ponti included, did ensure that David received his rightful dues but the experience with Sam left him with a dislike of the breed. His opinion was in no way improved by the behaviour of Dino de Laurentiis during his involvement in *Mutiny on the Bounty*. Dino's telephone calls were picked up by David's short-wave radio allowing him to witness Dino's double dealing on the venture.

The machinations of the typical Hollywood producer are well summed up by Dean Rossel in this passage from *Boston After Dark*:

Motion pictures seem to attract the wildest, the most megalomaniac, the most neurotic personalities. For the producers and distributors it is a high-tension business, where the chance of financial reward is so great that a man is usually ready, even willing, to risk any tactic to get

his "deal" through the front office. Gossip, wheeling and dealing, chiselling, fraud, inflated rhetoric, international plane hopping, extravagant promises, publicity stunts and Byzantine contracts of book length are the accepted pattern of existence.

Yet even with all these armaments at a producer's disposal David felt that ultimately he would have the upper hand.

"I listen to everything they have to say; I hear all their suggestions and ideas. I simply stand with my arms crossed and answer, "Yes" to anything I am asked.

"Why do you reply 'yes' to everything they ask if you don't agree with it?" I asked.**"Well you see Babe,"** he said laughing, **"Once I am on set and direction has started I can then do anything I want to do, I'm 'King Pin'"** ... dramatic pause ... **"they can't really turn round and fire me can they!"**

4 DIRECTION – DAVID'S REEL OBSESSION

Why they [studio executives] occasionally say yes [to a script] is far beyond my knowledge. But when they do, the producer has a "go" project.

And then, oh then, enters the director. This takes a tremendous amount of time – because the directors you want are always busy. A rule of mine is this: there are always three hot directors and one of them is always David Lean. Today it's Lucas, Spielberg and Lean. A few years back Coppola, Friedkin and Lean. A few years before that Penn, Nichols and Lean.

Well you can't get them. Many producers don't even want them – the more powerful the director, the less so the producer.

WILLIAM GOLDMAN, 1983

ABOVE: **Donatellos for** *Lawrence of Arabia* **and** *The Bridge on the River Kwai.*

ABOVE: **David's honorary life membership from the Directors Guild of America,**

FAR LEFT: **Academy Awards for** *Lawrence of Arabia* **and** *The Bridge on the River Kwai.*

LEFT: **David's BAFTA fellowship award.**

OPPOSITE: **"Hot" and dusty director on** *Lawrence.*

ABOVE: David views
perfection in France.

DAVID DIRECTED at all times – even when he wasn't making a film. At the Moulin, our home in France, David breakfasted on a small terrace leading from the bedroom. Many mornings I would find him looking intently in one particular direction. He would move his head from side-to-side or slightly shift his chair while staring at one point, then lift his finger as if measuring a distance.

"What are you measuring?" I asked him finally. "What are you looking at?"

The disturbance was a telegraph pole that offended his eye. After many days of deliberation he finally announced, in no uncertain terms, that a cypress tree had to be planted to obliterate the guilty representative of France Telecom. Not a small tree but one which needed the combined strength of seven swarthy Frenchman to cart up the hill. How they got it there he did not care, it just had to be done. Everyone looked at him in astonishment.

Film technicians are experienced when it comes to the precise needs of the director and his vision. A French building worker has much more pressing needs, lunch being cardinal. This did not concern the man who had moved armies through both the desert and the Siberian wastes. Finally, in 32 degrees of heat, sweat pouring off

LEFT: Setting up success on *Kwai*.

sense. Fortunately, one of Noël's many talents was to recognize talent in others and, seeking the best available crew to help him with *In Which We Serve*, he turned to David. Kay Walsh, his then wife, encouraged David to demand a better position and the shy perfectionist was launched on his journey.

When David was awarded the American Film Institute's Life Achievement Award in 1990, the term **"poet of the far horizon"** was freely used: "poet" because of the wonderful shorthand he used to evoke emotion and "far horizon" for the atmospheric wide shots that he choreographed so brilliantly in his films. Combine these concepts and you have David.

them, the workers managed to haul the tree in place and stand it in the hole they had dug for it. Proudly they raised a thumb to ask, "Is it OK?"

"No," said the director. "Two inches to the left and I'll raise my hand when I want you to stop."

As noon approached, the heaving became more animated. Finally, the exact position was agreed, a new hole dug and the tree planted, all to ensure that a clear, uninterrupted view of nature would greet the perfectionist every morning.

The origins of David's directing skills lay in his passion for cinema, his love of photography and a desire to let the world share his experiences. At thirty-four, he was the highest paid and most experienced editor in the business, he could have remained in the cutting room where he could manipulate the pace of life at any time of day or night. But the 12x12-foot room bound this personal fiefdom and the walls limited his vision. He wanted more.

Like many others in the film industry, David wanted to direct, but his shyness and his belief that he was not worthy of such a role held him back until Noël Coward presented him with an opportunity that was too good to miss. Coward was a great theatrical talent but his knowledge of the technicalities of film production was not as acute as his theatrical

Where did his creative power come from, this "reel obsession"? Perhaps it came about because he had a grey side to him. If we examine his childhood, everything that surrounded him was black and white. He felt different; on the one hand, this pleased him as he went into his own world of make-believe; on the other, why couldn't he excel like his brother and his father? Many of the films he chose to direct and the stories he told so well were about flawed characters, like him. Something within him rebelled against boring convention, so he inadvertently started to explore that unconventional streak that fuelled him; at the same time he got rid of his inadequacies by throwing them at the characters in his films. This, together with his masterly choreography, made his films unique. Directing in itself is unconventional, it is artistic. So it is possible to see the loner, the adventurer, seeking to find himself in his films.

Isolated by vast landscapes – a speck on the horizon – those flawed characters in his films grapple with romance and all the major problematic components of life.

He loved the art of film-making. It was more important to him than anything, including his relationships or his possessions. It was his way of bringing magic to an audience, scenes he saw himself which he

OPPOSITE, MAIN PICTURE:
Seeking the solution
on *Lawrence*.

OPPOSITE, INSET: Sam Spiegel
and Willie Wyler visiting
a *Lawrence* location.

ABOVE: David visits Willie
Wyler on the set of *Ben Hur*.

RIGHT: Directing in the desert.

wanted to share. He often said to aspiring directors, **"Do you dream?"** He didn't mean do you dream as at night, but he was enquiring about daydreams. It was these daydreams that gave him the insight into character that is witnessed and fulfilled in his films. But no one knew better than he did that dreams were not enough:

I think one of the most difficult things about a director's job is that he's got to be a bit of a dreamer and dreamers don't generally go hand in hand with practical people and if you're going to be a director you've certainly got to be practical. It's not an airy-fairy business at all, it's a hard job of work.

David was obsessed by movie-making; the way a shot was composed, the way one shot joined another to become a sequence. The music joins the dialogue, then the sound effects are added. All these elements come together and turn a beam of light into the transportation of an audience into another world. The satisfaction of seeing a whole audience engrossed in your work.

David mastered this art and couldn't understand those people who were not excited by this wonderful medium. He marvelled at the excellence of Orson Welles's *Citizen Kane*, watching it countless times. Kane himself – yet another powerful but flawed hero – fascinated him. He was able to immerse himself completely in these celluloid relationships.

That his films were nominated for fifty-seven Oscars and won twenty-eight, was a source of immense satisfaction to David. Yet, he never understood how certain people criticized work that they themselves could not create. He did not see why, if a film moved an audience, some felt it their job to pull it apart, to destroy it, often for minor reasons or jealousies. As David told *Time* Magazine: "The critics are intellectuals, I've always been frightened of intellectuals. The only people who don't give a damn, who are out there giving their opinions, are the critics."

It was this pack of wolves that drove David to despair. Pauline Kael, who had obviously not fallen for David's manly countenance, wrote in her *New Yorker* review of *Ryan's Daughter*:

As a director, he is a super technician, and probably he doesn't really have anything he wants to do in movies except command the technology. He probably enjoys working his characteristic gentleman-technician's tastefully colossal style … For years, during the making of a Lean film, publicity people send out photographs of the handsome director standing in the cities he has built, and then the movies arrive and he never seems to have figured out what to do in those sets. Will the public buy twinkling orgasms and cosmetic craftsmanship?

Not content with her written attack, at a meeting of film critics at the Algonquin Hotel in New York where David was a guest, she continued her tirade. David finally replied, "You won't be content until you've reduced me to filming in black and white on 16mm." To which she replied "We'll give you colour." David found it profoundly shocking to be challenged by a roomful of strangers who bore him so much malice. He had coped with bad reviews before, but being confronted in this way was devastating. The critics had conceived a forum where they could meet directors face-to-face but the sessions had turned into bear-baiting contests. Forty magazine critics versus one director – they having three movies to review each week while David had taken three years to make this one picture. He was in a state of shock.

I thought, what the hell am I doing if my work is as bad as all this? I didn't want to do another film. I thought, I'll do something else. I went travelling round the world and didn't make a film for fourteen years. I thought, what's the point?

ABOVE: **David captures
the desert.**

OPPOSITE: **David's recce shot
sets the scale for** *Lawrence*.

The point is that, notwithstanding the critics, David's work was a tremendous inspiration to other film-makers. This was aptly proved by the wonderful tribute Steven Spielberg made to him at the American Film Institute in 1990:

We've come here today to honour and say thank you to Sir David Lean. But I feel that I'm here today on a more personal basis because David brought me here and in fact you could say he bought me my ticket, because it was two of his films, *The Bridge on the River Kwai* and *Lawrence of Arabia*, that most made me want to be a film-maker. The scope and audacity of those films filled my dreams with unlimited possibilities. *Lawrence* gives me the same spark of inspiration now and thanks to the restoration its inspiration can be, to all of us, perpetual.

We have to look back so that we keep looking forward, and whenever I turn around I only see *Lawrence*. Every tool used to make movies was used in the making of *Lawrence of Arabia*, used and abused, sometimes past what we might have thought possible. The performances, the editing, the score, the costume design, the production design and Robert Bolt's screenplay which, as far as I'm concerned, is the best ever written, all these elements were put together by David Lean with consummate brilliance and absolute economy. There is nothing extraneous in *Lawrence* or in any Lean picture. There is nothing ever wasted. Every shot is a tool that unlocks the plot and every image an echo of the heart. So for me *Lawrence* is somewhere between a cornerstone and a grail. I was inspired the first time I saw it. It made me feel puny. It still makes me feel puny, and that's just one measure of its greatness, because it's a continued inspiration and it's cutting the rest of us down to size.

Writers often reflect on the intensity of their first reading experiences. They remember what it was like the first time they encountered Dickens or Hemingway or Mark Twain or Thomas Hardy, and I felt and remember that kind of intensity about all of David Lean's movies. David Lean makes movies that are the equivalent of great novels. With one difference – when you read it's your imagination that creates the imagery, but with films you have to trust the director's imagination and if he's a good director then you don't betray that trust, but **if you're a great director like David you can even go past it and put pictures on the screen that not even our imaginations can anticipate.**

ONE Steven Spielberg is worth many plane-loads of arrogant critics, who often arrive at screenings late, therefore missing the vital opening and establishing scenes. David would say, "**Grab an audience in the first three minutes and they are yours for hours.**" He was incensed by the late arrival of the critics who missed

David's shot of the "far horizon",
Lawrence of Arabia.

the first five to ten minutes of the film. How could these people judge a piece of work when they had missed the beginning, the crucial scene that constituted the bedrock for the rest of the production?

He therefore ordered that no one could enter a screening once the picture had started, a policy he even followed at home! Consequently Lawrence Kasdan, the writer of *Raiders of the Lost Ark* and *Return of the Jedi* who then directed *Body Heat* and *The Big Chill,* hit a rich seam when he told this story during the AFI tribute:

In early 1963, my brother and I rode a bus for ninety blocks down Miami Beach to see *Lawrence of Arabia* on the Lincoln Mall. We arrived seven minutes late for the matinee. My brother, who at nineteen was older and wiser than I, refused to go into the theatre. Instead, we loitered in the streets for six hours so we could see the movie from the start. As I endured the long wait, I thought my brother was crazy. But when the show was over, I knew I had done the right thing. As I stumbled from the theatre, having seen the whole movie, **I had a new hero. It was not T. E. Lawrence, but David Lean.** I emerged a most unusual creature, a fourteen-year-old boy who knew what he wanted to do with the rest of his life.

David loved this story. It was an example of the great respect Americans have for movies, he often said "The British loathe success where as the Americans admire success." The Americans love movies and they shared his obsession. However, although he made films that were financed with American funds, he only ever made one very short sequence in an American studio, which was for *The Greatest Story Ever Told.*

Their technicians fascinated him. They worked fast and loved their work. It was quite an eye-opener for someone who spent so much of his time making the British technician and British actor such a major force in international movies but why the British became uninterested he could never understand.

A word most frequently used about David is "concentration". Katharine Hepburn says that in her experience "only Howard Hughes had an equal ability to concentrate." Anthony Havelock-Allan who, as well as producing many of David's films, also produced Franco Zeffirelli's *Romeo and Juliet* says,

"David is Michelangelo, total absorption. Zeffirelli is Leonardo, doing everything – costumes, plays. David is one hundred per cent film man. One hundred per cent film man."

ABOVE LEFT: **Petra Gorge in Jordan.**

ABOVE: **A still of Wadi Rumm from** *Lawrence.*

OPPOSITE: **David's recce shot of Wadi Rumm.**

ABOVE LEFT AND RIGHT: On the set of *Ryan's Daughter*, David demonstrates how to do a scene, which Robert Mitchum does.

LEFT: Gregory Peck, who wanted the Mitchum part in *Ryan's Daughter*.

ABOVE AND RIGHT: Writer Robert
Bolt watches as David directs
his wife, Sarah Miles, in the
wedding scene on the set
of *Ryan's Daughter*.

OPPOSITE, TOP: The influence – Robert Flaherty's
brilliant documentary *Man of Aran* (1934).

LEFT AND ABOVE: The original storyboard for the scene.

OVERLEAF: The movie final and the publicity material for the film.

The Storm Sequence from *Ryan's Daughter*

Another enormous wave picks up the tangled
mess of wood and rope and smashes it down again.
Boxes come adrift. We see one hammered on the
rocks. It flies apart. Rifles.

—Robert Bolt, Screenplay, Page 144

Une énorme vague soulève de nouveau le fouillis
de bois et de cordes et l'abat aussitôt. Des caisses s'en
détachent. Nous en voyons une qui se brise contre
les rochers. Elle éclate en morceaux. Des fusils.

Otra enorme ola recoje el compuso lío de cuerdas
y madera y lo lanza violentamente otra vez en
golpe destructor. Flotan cajas a la deriva. Vemos una
que se esprella contra las rocas. Se abre en pedazos.
Fusiles.

Noch eine gewaltige Welle ergreift den
verschlungenen Mischmash von Holz und Seilen
und schmettert ihn wieder hinunter. Kisten treiben
auseinander. Wir sehen wie eine auf die Felsen
geschleudert wird. Sie zerschmettert. Gewehre.

Un' altra onda gigantesca solleva il groviglio
di assi e di corda e poi lo scaglia di nuovo verso il
basso. Casse alla deriva. Una va a spattere con violenza
contro gli scogli. Si fracassa. Fucili.

もう一つの大きな波が縄と木片のめちゃめちゃになった塊を
さらい、又猛烈な勢で下にたたきつけた。多数の木箱が漂流
して来る。その中の一つが岩にたたきつけられ粉々に飛散す
るのが見える。銃だ！

A new film by David Lean
Ryan's Daughter

David with cast and crew viewing rushes of *Oliver Twist* (1948). LEFT: Anthony Newley (the Artful Dodger); CENTRE: Alec Guinness (Fagin); and RIGHT: Robert Newton (Bill Sikes).

5 CAST

In those four frames there is the
difference between actor and star.

DAVID LEAN

MICHAEL CAINE ONCE ASKED David what the difference was between a good actor and a star. David replied, "I can't tell you as a director but I can tell you as an editor. When a good actor finishes a line I cut but when a star delivers the line I leave it four extra frames. In those four frames there is the difference between actor and star – an unknown difference but it is definitely there."

David was not particularly influenced by the star system. He was more interested in unknown actors; he immediately recognized screen presence. He was responsible for launching some of the greatest actors in film history: Richard Attenborough in his first film, *In Which We Serve*; John Mills and Alec Guinness in *Great Expectations* (1946); Peter O'Toole and Omar Sharif in *Lawrence of Arabia* – all went on to be international stars. One of the most requested clips in the British Film Institute Library is for the screen test that Albert Finney did for the role of Lawrence. Fearing stardom, he turned down the part, which was also offered to Marlon Brando.

Yet David had seen a quality in Peter O'Toole that outweighed all other casting considerations. Peter's portrayal of Lawrence is probably one of the most memorable experiences of the cinema. Why he did not win an Oscar is beyond my comprehension.

The contenders for the role of "Lawrence" included Albert Finney (LEFT), who even did a screen test, and Marlon Brando (OPPOSITE, FAR RIGHT), but when David met Peter O'Toole (ABOVE AND OPPOSITE) he instantly found his solution.

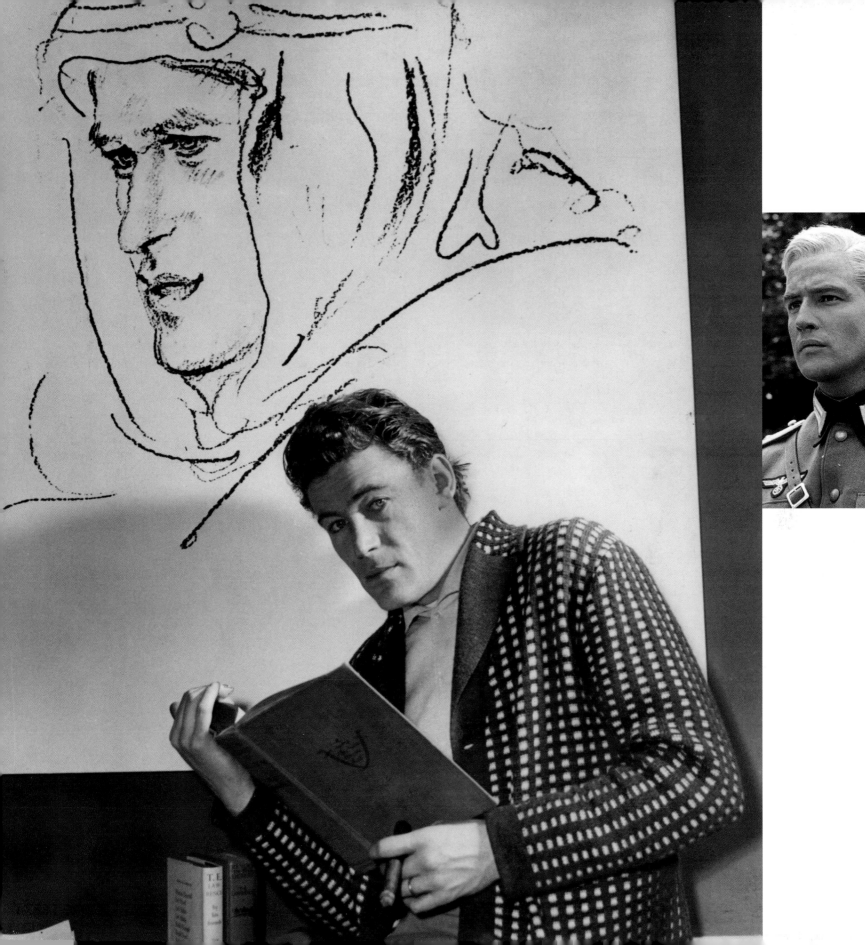

Among the many positive elements David brought to his casting, one particularly successful one was the great friendship that grew between Peter and Omar. How the Irishman brought up in Leeds and the sophisticated Egyptian would have ever met without being confined in the Jordanian desert for many, many months would be hard to imagine.

I remember during the AFI tribute to David there was a satellite link to Omar and Peter who were sitting around a fire in a Surrey pub. Obviously, they had stayed up late rather than getting up early, and were in a very jovial mood. They spoke movingly of their love and respect for David, but what also emanated from this interview was their great understanding of one another. Peter spoke first:

It is no secret that first thing in the morning you do not find me at my best. It is no secret, certainly not to you and to many other of my film world colleagues. However, you do not find me at my worst either. You do, however, find me.

When you have absorbed all these uniquely deserved and proper plaudits and when you are fed up to the teeth of saying, "too kind, most loyal, everybody very good and gracious." Now, I can say this because of my abiding affection and deepest respect. David, it would please me and the entire cinema world if you were simply to get up off your arse and go out and make another picture! God Bless.

The cameras then homed in on Omar, who said:

It's very difficult doing this because you can see us and we can't see you, but I'm trying to imagine what's going on at the moment where you are.

Everybody's had de-caf coffee with "Sweet and Low". Some of you are sipping diet champagne, I suppose, with whole-wheat petits-fours and people have been saying wonderful things about your great achievements in the film industry and pretty soon somebody's going to get up and say, "Ladies and Gentlemen, will you please rise for Sir David Lean."

Well at this point I would like to, just for a minute, be a director and tell you what to do, David, as you've always told me what to do.

When they start applauding, standing ovation and all, you get slowly up, David, don't hurry and stand absolutely still. Wait for it all to subside.

Then take half a step towards the mike and hold the silence for a little while – you've got them there, David – and then with your inimitable accent, say what everybody is waiting to hear, "You ain't seen nothin' yet."

After filming *Lawrence*, Peter said:

The most important influence in my life has been David Lean. I graduated in Lean, took my BA in Lean, worked day and night for two years. Lean gave me discipline and tolerance … And I learned the hard way. **Mind you, *Lawrence* wasn't a film. IT WAS AN EXPERIENCE.**

All they paid me for Lawrence was a hundred quid a week – buttons for me and Omar. Actually, we'd have paid David Lean two hundred quid a week just to do it for him … David's a bit remote; maybe that's the trouble.

If David appeared remote, this was not because he was cold but more because of his total concentration when directing a movie. David could and did spend years perfecting a script; it was this time that allowed him to perfect the characters and the framework. By then the film was already formed in his head, the characters were so clearly defined in his mind that he even knew what underwear they were wearing. As Noël Coward said, "Even if you don't show them eating breakfast, you ought to know what they had for breakfast."

Consequently, casting should have been easier, but it was not. By the time he had finished the script, although he had a perfect vision of the characters, he then had to find the right actor to mirror his exact image. When casting, he would ask, "Now, count to ten, living or dead, who could play this part?" The first appearance of an actor on screen was of paramount importance to all his films; it is here that the immediate understanding of a character begins. David respected the art of an actor, but it didn't necessarily mean that he had to become friends with them.

Alec Guinness has often been quoted as saying that he owed David his career. Although, who owed whom which career can be debated. It was a relationship that dated back to the early 1940s when David was looking for an alternative to Noël Coward's scripts, having become deeply concerned that he was filming "staged productions" rather than capturing the visual cinematographic impact that would become his trademark. He rediscovered Dickens after being dragged by Kay Walsh to Alec's stage production of *Great Expectations* in a theatre near to her flat by Marylebone Station during the war. David remembered this performance when he was casting for his version of the classic novel and cast Alec as Herbert Pocket, which began a very close and fruitful relationship for many of the Lean films.

It was, none the less, a very difficult relationship. David often wanted Alec to appear in productions for which Alec felt he was not suitable.

Alec was such a good actor, that one could argue forever trying to decide which character was his best achievement. Perhaps his most famous is Colonel Nicholson in *The Bridge on the River Kwai*. However director and actor argued incessantly about the interpretation of the character. Many of the Colonel's mannerisms were, in fact, David's and not Alec's. The stroking of the bridge in *Kwai* is carefully described in the original script and illustrates David's very tactile nature. He felt that the man who had built the bridge, even though it was for his enemies, would have loved to just touch the fine workmanship "as [you would] a Chippendale". Was this part of David's inheritance from the Tangye side of the family or his intrinsic sensuality? Probably both.

Alec was so versatile. David recognized this versatility in the early films they made together, casting him in the widely differing roles of Herbert Pocket in *Great Expectations* and Fagin in *Oliver Twist*. Over the years the range became remarkable. Alec's appearances in

Lawrence and *Zhivago* were not lead parts, but key roles and, again, they reflected David. Alec's superb acting ability enabled him to do this although he was probably not aware of it.

By the time David came to make *A Passage to India* (1984) Alec had already reaped the benefits of his appearances in the *Star Wars* trilogy. Possibly he felt he knew best. After all, there had been many "Lean" years – David had not made a film for fourteen years.

They differed strongly about Godbole, the character Alec played in the film, and unfortunately the dispute became public knowledge. They were like a pair of heavyweights slowly grinding each other to the ground. It's difficult to believe these two great friends had drifted apart. The estrangement appeared to continue after David's death. When I asked Alec to participate in David's memorial service, he refused. I do not know whether this was because of their differences, however; I'm inclined to believe that it was due more to Alec's shyness. He was a very private person. I noticed that he discreetly slipped into the cathedral and sat near the back, not wishing to be seen. I totally understand. In his book *My Name Escapes Me*, Alec wrote:

> I had to balance my thoughts as best I could. Pushing aside my bad recollections of David's extreme unpleasantness in latter years but remembering the enchanting, affable, exciting man he was in the days of making *Great Expectations* and *Oliver Twist*. He could still switch on the charm even in his last years but I had grown mistrustful of it. We each did our best, I think, to repair our damaged friendship but it didn't really work out. I needed someone with whom I could laugh (not David's strongest point) and he depended so much, it seemed to me, on sycophants. But he was marvellously generous with his riches. The car left St Paul's behind in the fading light. I wished David eternal happiness, as I have always done since the day he died.

With John Mills, on the other hand, David retained both a warm friendship and a smooth working relationship. They first worked together on *In Which We Serve* and from then a friendship blossomed that never died. One of Johnny's most memorable parts for David came after a long gap. David was living in Rome at the time and as Johnny and his wife, Mary, were also visiting the city they all spent an evening together. "David, what's been going on with you?" asked Mary over dinner. "You know you haven't worked with Johnny for years. Isn't there something in *Ryan's Daughter* for him?" And David looked at Johnny and took the longest pause – it went on forever – and said finally, "Johnny do you think you could play a dumb village idiot?" Johnny replied, "No problem, David – type casting."

At the AFI Life Achievement Award to David, Johnny said there were not many occasions when he would fly for over twenty-two hours for an

LEFT: Alec
Guinness and
David reflecting
upon Godbole
during the making
of *A Passage
to India* (1984).

OPPOSITE: *Ryan's Daughter:*
John Mills is "typecast"
as village idiot.

RIGHT: **Bill Holden apologizes**
for his "baskets of fruit"
expedition during the making
of *The Bridge on the River Kwai.*

unpaid engagement but for David it was different. A few years after David's death Johnny appeared on the London stage and thereafter was invited to be a guest on Clive Anderson's television chat show. He continually wanted to talk about David, as he believed he had influenced his career. Unfortunately, Clive declined to pick up on Johnny's comments, preferring to keep to his prepared line of questioning.

If David liked actors, it was only those actors that he felt he could relate to as people. Those who were unpretentious and those who could visualize a character. This was difficult to quantify. Often he would not ask an actor to read the part in a casting session; instead he would just prefer to talk to them. This enabled the actor in question to be more at ease with the situation and, moreover, allowed David to feel more at ease.

Before one of these casting sessions David probably felt more nervous than the actor waiting for his interview. These sessions could, occasionally, last for up to two hours. By the end of such a session he already knew whether the actor "had it or not".

When directing a film, David rarely dined with actors. For the most part this was because he reserved this time for himself in order to concentrate on the next day's shooting. He did not want to be diverted.

What David did not need from an actor was pomposity. After all, it was hard enough working day in and day out with a long schedule. What he looked for was the professionalism that actors brought to the screen – their total dedication. He particularly admired these qualities in William Holden and Katharine Hepburn. Bill Holden also made him laugh; he had a wicked sense of humour away from the camera.

David told this story of Bill. Producer Sam Spiegel was making one of his rare visits to the steamy location in Ceylon during the shooting of *The Bridge on the River Kwai* and was ensconced in his air-conditioned suite at the hotel. At a dinner that evening Sam's wife, Betty, turned to a slightly inebriated Bill and told him how totally exhausted Sam was from his journey. This incensed Bill. "Whaddya mean, Sam's exhausted! There's David up at the bridge, working his arse off in a hundred per cent humidity and you're telling me Sam's exhausted!" He ranted on for a while and then said to Betty, "You know what, Betty, you're a 'c—t'." Betty complained to Sam while Doreen Hawkins, Jack Hawkins's wife, tried to calm Bill down. Bill replied, "You know what, Doreen you're a c—t too!" At this point an enraged Sam stood up, as if he was going to punch Bill. Suddenly he stopped his actions in midstream because if he had knocked Bill out he would have lost the main star in the film, which would have cost the production thousands of dollars per day! Meanwhile, Bill's wife, Ardis, began to cry, at the same time trying to silence him. Turning on his wife, the actor added, "And what's more, Ardis, you're a c—t too!" Bill finally realized that he had gone too far and walked out.

The following day at the bridge location the usually professional and punctual movie star failed to make an appearance when he was called for a shot. Bill was nowhere to be seen. David and the crew got on with another scene that didn't involve him, and at lunchtime a very apologetic and hungover Bill Holden appeared and, full of remorse, explained to David what had happened. "I behaved badly at dinner last night, I'm afraid. I called all the women at the table 'c—s', including my own wife. I've been out searching Colombo high and low all morning for flowers but since I couldn't find any flowers I bought all the c—ts baskets of fruit instead."

Katharine Hepburn became one of David's closest friends. That friendship remained throughout his life. They only worked together once, on *Summer Madness* (*Summertime*, as it was titled in the United

States), which David directed in Venice in 1955. From then on, they often spoke on the telephone and whenever David was in America he visited her. Their admiration was mutual. Said Katharine:

David has an enthusiasm for working in film far beyond one's imagination, whose capacity for work has no end, whose determination is to produce the best possible result, to whom nothing matters – discomfort, exhaustion – so long as it contributes to a perfect result. **My admiration for David is infinite**.

Celia Johnson had a particular quality that David would always admire; she had a natural talent; she was well balanced and totally unaffected. Although he always wished everyone in his productions would believe that the movie was the most important aspect in their lives, he would allow Celia favours denied to others. When she demanded to be released from the set on Saturdays so that she could be with her doctor husband, she would be given leave. She touched him enormously. I noticed that when we ran any of the three of the films that starred Celia – *In Which We Serve* (1942), *This Happy Breed* (1944) and *Brief Encounter* (1945) – David's tears would fall unashamedly at her excellence.

Casting his two actress wives, Kay Walsh and Ann Todd, in his films took its toll and he vowed never to do it again. He felt that by not being too close or having an intimate relationship with his actresses he was able to get a much better performance from them. This was certainly the case with Julie Christie and Geraldine Chaplin in *Doctor Zhivago*. Their dramatic performances helped to make the film one of the most successful and greatest love stories ever brought to the screen.

Incidentally, Julie reminds me of David's niece Sarah Lean. She spent much time with him and he cared deeply for her. In some respects, their relationship is similar to the one I have with his great-niece Lucy who originally started writing this book with me but she moved to New York to marry the love of her life.

When David wasn't filming, the cast in his private life were mainly people who came from the industry. One member of this cast was Marlon Brando.

David had offered him roles in his films but, unfortunately, for one reason or Marlon was never able to accept. One part he did get, however, was to participate as a guest, at David's fourth marriage. One of the other wedding guests was Barbara Hutton, the Woolworth's heiress who gave away the bride, Leila.

David's friends were few and far between but Vita and Victor Hohenloe were very close to him. They had met in Rome during the time David lived there. They were great fun, utterly unpretentious and totally beautiful people, their relationship I cherish now. Any book about David's personal life would be incomplete without mention of them.

Another very close friend of David's was Group-Captain Leonard Cheshire, VC. Such an important ranking would normally have frightened David but in this case not at all. Leonard had been awarded the Victoria Cross for completing a hundred bombing missions, often at low altitude, on heavily defended German targets. He was also one of the British observers on the atomic bombing in Nagasaki. Afterwards he dedicated his life to charity, creating homes for the terminally ill across the world. Leonard was a very private person and did not often talk about his experiences during the war but he did confide them to his great friend, David. When he entered a room, it was as if a metaphysical spirit had entered. The entire atmosphere of that room became very calm and peaceful. I likened him to a prophet.

This quiet authority is also present in Kevin Brownlow who wrote David's authorized biography. While researching his book Kevin spent many weeks with David who was impressed by his knowledge and passion. A certain passion combined with imagination seemed to be the common currency that David demanded in those close to him.

In the introduction to his biography on David, Kevin wrote:

I know this will not be the last biography of David Lean – I hope it won't – but I suspect it will be the most affectionate. I cannot judge whether I have done justice to his life. He has certainly enriched mine.

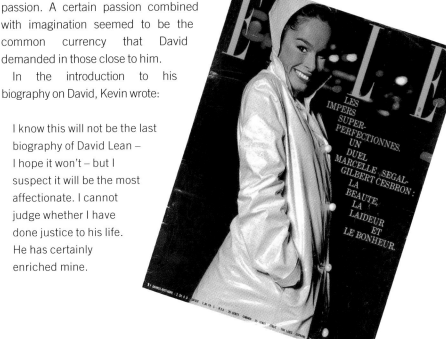

6 TRANSPORTATION AND LOCATION

I suppose I'm kind of a nut in a way. The most important thing in my life is my work. I like doing films in rather wild places. I find wild places exciting. I like showing things on the screen that people in the normal way don't see.

FROM "DAVID LEAN – A SELF-PORTRAIT", BBC, SEPTEMBER 30, 1971.

MADE WHILE HE WAS CUTTING *RYAN'S DAUGHTER*.

DAVID'S FILMS FIRED the imagination of audiences worldwide. Subconsciously, he brought foreign cultures into a basically insular Western society. He not only transported himself but took us all with him into his land of make-believe. In his personal life he made physical journeys with his friends, wives and mistresses but through his films he made spiritual and emotional journeys. Few film-makers today have the ability or passion to stretch their audience's eye and mind in the way that David did. He always believed that a film-maker had to absorb his or her audience completely into a story otherwise there would be no magical journey from the drudgery of everyday life into the fantasy of the movies. That is how it all started for him.

Within the confines of a small cinema he, through his films, made the world a smaller place.

I believe that David succeeded as a director because of his tortured, intense relationship with himself: a flawed man relating to the flawed characters in the films he chose to direct; the single, lonely figure reluctantly battling against harsh events. Such were, Colonel Nicholson in *Kwai*, Yuri in *Doctor Zhivago* and, of course, T.E. Lawrence. These characters mirrored him. Although I am as certain as I can be that he did not choose these subjects or characters to release

ABOVE: **A memento that we picked together from a tree in Tahiti.**

RIGHT: **The wonders of Tahiti.**

himself from his own emotions, inevitably this happened and it was easy to escape into celluloid. He must have seen himself over and over again when adapting *The Seven Pillars of Wisdom* for the movie. T.E. Lawrence says, **"If I could not assume their character, I could at least conceal my own."**

When he talked about the desert, David said, **"I suppose it was really the first time that I realized the world was mine and that I needn't be fenced in. It knocked me out."** It was there that he not only discovered his love for these locations but also began to discover himself. It was there that he found a sense of belonging, a sense of space, of inspiration and a feeling of finally having found that elusive path for which he had always been searching. It was also there that he found as a loner a convergence of parallel values, a sense of kinship with Lawrence. It was this film that forged a bond between David, the film-maker and Lawrence the warrior. *Lawrence of Arabia* was not just a tribute to T.E. Lawrence from David but an act of friendship. He said that his experiences in the desert made him acutely aware of how small the human being is against the backdrop of its unending hugeness. He loved the simplicity, leaving behind all Western conventions with their restrictions. His spirit was freed in this atmosphere. The desert seemed to allow him to quit his English self;

before, there had been within him a contempt, not for other men, but for all they did and this left him with loneliness.

"Getting to know you, getting to know all about you ..." That wonderful Rogers and Hammerstein song from *The King and I* is going round and round in my head. I feel a little like a psychologist as I write this book. I did when David and I were together. I had to be, in order to understand the man. He recognized his failings in life but found these increasingly difficult to deal with since the responsibility of film-making took over. He once said about himself, "the real limitations are within myself. The money, the camera, the actors and the technicians are there. I also have a pen and a blank sheet of paper." I think the great "transportation" and understanding of himself certainly happened in the desert but it was much earlier, in his teens, that the tough climb commenced although, at the time, he probably was not aware of it. His "heightened senses", especially his "sixth sense" – a combination of intuition and spirituality – together with his vision, started it all.

Being lonely, he became a dreamer and confided all his dreams to the camera. "I wanted to talk to people, but I only let it out to the camera. It's a funny thing to say but its true. The camera became my friend."

The eyes yearned for more; the lens had to get bigger. They stretched to the cinema.

OPPOSITE AND THIS PAGE:
The unending hugeness
of the desert and the
smallness of man.

I could actually smell the cinema in Reading. I had sneaked in just as the lights were dimming. That was a magic moment. The glow of light from the orchestra pit, the dim outline of the conductor. I can almost see myself as if in a close shot. Fourteen years old, a stiff collar and tie, tense with anticipation. Then, a sudden sweep of velvet curtains revealing the white screen which throws the conductor into silhouette as his arms descend and the orchestra crashes out.

Imagine his memory retaining that "close up" for many decades.

So, that crucial present of the camera started to stretch the eye and when his father took him to Pompeii the burning curiosity began to build within him. He yearned to learn about new cultures and when an opportunity presented itself to him, he was off. Railway stations and steam trains excited him as a child and that excitement never left him. There they were catalogued in his head and used again and again in almost all his films. "I suppose it is the small boy in me," he said, "I think they are wonderful subjects for movies. They're almost alive."

A little later he discovered cruise ships and adored watching the sea from the deck of a ship. A bird of prey in flight moved him and then there was the aeroplane; in fact, anything and everything that carried him away from Croydon to unfamiliar and exotic landscapes. His appetite was huge and he remained hungry until the end of his life.

His "sixth sense" was heightened by his visits to India. In the late 1950s when he was editing *Kwai* in Paris, he thought about India a lot.

I love it so much outside the towns and even now I am still a little frightened by this West of ours. Paris is so damned clinical. It's like a bone without any marrow in it. There's such a show of affection and warmth but very little devotion. The waiters, the servants and all the rest of them are so brittle and I long for a sweet Indian bearer with all his faults. I shall go back as soon as I can and one day I may buy that small house in view of Nanga Parbat and grow those crisp Kashmiri apples.

He was at one with himself there. I travelled there with him and observed how he marvelled at the landscape and the light. He loved the people. It was so touching that he wanted to share his excitement with me and it was as if it was his first visit. He had taken every woman close to him to visit the same countries that had fired him; they each visited the same sights – the Pyramids, the Taj Mahal and Tahiti but it was as if he had forgotten. He had of course erased these visits from his head as he had erased the women: CUT.

OPPOSITE: The beginning of the magic moment in the cinema.

BELOW: A far cry from Croydon.

BOTTOM: Imagining magic moments in India.

We travelled the subcontinent by car, because David insisted that it was the only way to see the real India. Life is on the road as traders go to and fro from one city to another and I was captivated with the enormous amount of traffic, few cars but traffic jams of pack animals carrying large loads of cargo wrapped up in enormous white round bundles resembling laundry bags.

The first part of our journey was from Delhi south to Agra. I noticed that he was watching my reaction. People either love or hate India and usually the hate is because of the poverty. I felt an immediate empathy

David divining destiny.

AGRA

I N D I A

BAY OF
BENGAL

they formed a circle around us and just stared. David beckoned them to sit down beside us but they continued to stare. One of them spoke in Hindi to our driver, asking him if David was British and if he was, would he please take a message back to England and deliver it to the Queen, asking her please to come back!

Even now, I have the clearest images of our travels together. Every trip he made was likened to a recce for a film and contact sheets of holiday photographs were cropped, the cropping line marked in red pencil and a list was selected and numbered. Together with the negative, these were then sent to Venice to Mr. Tokazian who had printed all David's photographs for years. It was a ritual.

His description to me of his first visit to Egypt was memorable – he was a great storyteller and I would form pictures in my head as he was speaking. The journey to Cairo was long in those days and he was tired out and arrived at the hotel, which was very near to the Pyramids. His room was stuffy and he opened the windows. Suddenly, his tiredness vanished as he saw the Pyramids floodlit by a full moon. He rushed

with the people and I didn't just enjoy India, I fell in love with India. He took me to several historic places en route until finally I got my first glimpse of the Taj Mahal, which is mind blowing. I had to pinch myself and, yes, I was awake. I was not dreaming. The whole story connected to that memorial is so emotional, it brings tears to one's eyes. David took many wonderful photographs as he had done on so many other occasions. It never ceased to amaze him. Suddenly, he noticed an American taking a photograph; he grimaced, and mumbling something, walked over to the gentleman. He returned almost giggling. He had kindly advised him that if he took the photograph from a different angle, he would get the right light on the marble and the photograph would be much improved. The man took umbrage and said, **"Who do you think you are, David Lean!"**

Distances are huge and there are not many places to stop. It is not too wise to eat at roadside restaurants so we used to picnic; we'd stop the car and eat in a deserted field with only the wonderful landscape surrounding us. Sometimes, we'd just sit in silence breathing in the peaceful aura. Villagers would appear from nowhere. On one occasion,

ABOVE LEFT: India – a favourite place.

ABOVE AND OPPOSITE: David always recropped
his photographs for a perfect print.

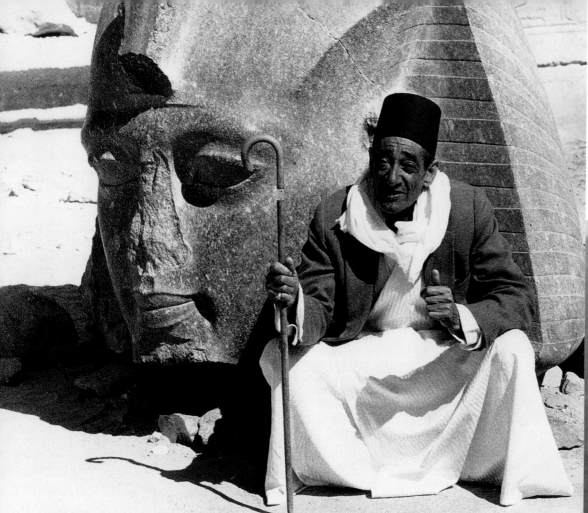

downstairs to ask the concierge if there was anyone to take him out there. His request granted, an Egyptian guide led him and they walked across the sand. From the calm of the evening, a dust storm sprang up and the two of them sat huddled together. "The sky became opaque and the effect with the full moon was immensely theatrical. The dust came in gusts and then paused and then, the opaque sky and the shape of the Pyramids. I've never lost the magic of that night," he said. From his description, neither have I.

Anthony Havelock-Allan first worked with David in 1942. He produced the early black and white movies with him and, later, *Ryan's Daughter*. He said "David was a marvellous storyteller, not only of the main scene but of each scene in a story. In another age he would have sat around a fire and told stories. He wouldn't have been a writer but a teller of tales."

After escaping from Croydon to the Studios, David never looked back. He travelled all the time. His greatest wish was to make films in those countries that he loved. To a great extent his wishes were granted but there was one disappointment. After first visiting Tahiti, he fell in love with Polynesia. "One does feel at the end of the world here," he said. I know David felt at one with the Tahitians. They are wonderful free spirits and they inhabit one of the most beautiful places God has put on this earth, at least for us. It is everything that David loved. The atoll, the motus, the huge palm leaves casting vast shadows on the white sand; the colourful people, the balmy temperature and the scent of the frangipani flowers.

It saddens me that he had picked his favourite location to make *The Bounty* and it never happened. He did everything in his power to make it happen. At the end of his life, he still talked about the script being one of the best ever written.

Well, it was not to be. It was "not written" but – *inshallah* – perhaps one day.

LEFT: David and Judy Davis filming the sexual awakening scene in *A Passage to India*.

7 PRODUCTION STAFF

I know I'm not terribly popular. I've come to terms with it. I'm not in pictures to promote my private personality; I'm in it for the joy of it.

FRED ZINNEMANN

THIS QUOTE COULD HAVE come from David, as he shared Fred's total dedication to film-making. Consequently they admired one another and were great friends. Both started in the film industry as technicians – Fred as assistant cameraman, David as editor; both made Oscar-winning movies and, thereafter, a few powerful but successful films. Both also worked with Robert Bolt, Fred directing *A Man for All Seasons*, which was adapted for the screen by the writer.

Both Fred and David were immensely focused while making a movie. A director is surrounded by hundreds of people during shooting but he is alone in the crowd as his task is to instruct virtually everyone.

Members of David's chosen family. ABOVE, TOP:
David and Freddie Young at the premiere of
Lawrence of Arabia, December 10, 1962.

ABOVE: Assistant directors David Tringham
and Mike Stevenson waiting for action.

OPPOSITE: Cameraman Freddie Young
shows Sarah Miles how to "toe the line."

"Making a movie is a collaborative effort, which means me telling a hundred and fifty-seven people exactly what to do," as film director Michael Winner has said.

Hence David, always the introvert, remained remote during production. To counteract his isolation, he surrounded himself with a "family" of technicians – an ironic position considering he shunned his natural family. He did not even attend his own mother's funeral because he was filming. During these "Lean years" his only contact with his relatives was to instruct that finance was in place to educate his brother's children and their families. However, much later in his life he did regain contact with them.

David's true family came from various technical departments within the industry, many of whom went on to work with David throughout his career. He called them his **"dedicated maniacs".** Like so many actors who worked with him, they became stars and Oscar-winners as a result of working on Lean productions.

David was a film technician who loved film-making. He cherished anyone who shared his passion. Unfortunately, during his life, being a film technician did not necessarily entail having a passion for film-making. Much of the reason for this was because of the way the technicians' union was run. There seemed to be a lack of understanding of cinema as art; and a resistance to the idea that the technicians' union should be organized in a very different way from other organizations.

Unfortunately, in a reaction to the bad treatment their members received in the 1930s, the union created a set of rules that stifled creativity rather than encouraged it. David's own work schedule in the late 1930s would have horrified the union in postwar Britain. Yet even with these restrictions there were some people who loved their work and skill – these were the people who became David's close working family.

David's crews had huge respect for him since he gave them such a vast canvas on which to practise and perfect their art. Yet, as usual, it was not always possible for the general to be friends with every sergeant under his command. This position was reserved for those who proved a singular dedication to the job. Among them were his assistant directors David Tringham, Mike Stevenson and Roy Stevens; his favoured cameraman, Freddie Young; the camera operator, Peter Newbrooke; and art director, John Box. Wyn Ryder, the sound editor, became David's ear, creating that sound magic which became the hallmark of David's films. And of course there was Maggie Unsworth, his great friend and continuity lady. **"I always work with the same people,"** David explained.

If a rehearsal's no damn good, I can say to the crew, "Now go off for twenty minutes and leave me with the

stand-ins." In the old days when something didn't work I'd have complete paralysis. But when I work with the same people I can do as I like. They won't think I'm loony.

Because he felt totally at ease with his chosen family, David ensured that his "maniacs" were always part of his productions in order to make his arduous task easier. His need for family extended to the kitchen. Like most armies, a film crew marches on its stomach and a British film crew needs those curious concoctions that remind them of home. From the heat of the desert, where water was driven over two hundred miles, to frozen wastes where his trucks sank into the lake, Phil Hobbs, the caterer and feeder of so many English film crews, was the purveyor of egg and bacon, fish and chips, sponge puddings and custard.

The Bridge on the River Kwai. After this production he worked with David on every subsequent picture and they were even together when they weren't making a movie.

It was Eddie who brought Richard Hough's book Captain Bligh and Mr Christian to David's attention and so began the unfortunate experience of the Mutiny on the Bounty project. Nevertheless, this period in Tahiti drew their friendship to a wonderful understanding of one another. Eddie understood that David was consumed by a desire to make the perfect film and he made every effort to ensure that this became possible.

Eddie is a larger-than-life Londoner: powerfully built, pugnacious, with a shock of hair and a florid face – a very "dedicated maniac". Whatever the contrast between their two backgrounds, they gelled from their first meeting on Kwai. Conditions in the jungle were pretty

Phil always tried to do his best for his charges and would try to serve David personally. This meant he would see David at his worst, first thing in the morning while bringing David his usual breakfast of eggs and bacon.

David suffered from low blood pressure; and it took him longer than most to co-ordinate himself in the morning. Consequently he was often a tad grumpy.

This story about Phil that David told me still makes me laugh. Each morning, usually before dawn, Phil brought David's breakfast to his caravan on a carefully laid tray. He had been in the kitchen for many hours by this time and was bright and chirpy. Now David, trying to rehearse a scene in his head, did not much appreciate chat in the morning, let alone chirpiness. One morning, David responded to Phil's bright "Good morning, sir," with a nod and a sort of grunt, and Phil, adopting his best camp manner, scolded, "Oh, deary me, someone's taken his ugly pills, hasn't he!" and flounced out.

Prop man Eddie Fowlie emerged from this family to become one of David's greatest friends. They originally met when Eddie worked on

hellish, the crew were getting restive and there had been a brief strike over who should be the assistant generator driver. In a bid to improve tempers in the incessant heat and humidity, David had taken to allowing the crew, after completing major shots, to swim in the river. On one such break, David dived in and surfaced next to his burly props man, who surveyed the situation and summed up their good fortune with a cheerful: "Bloody millionaire stuff!" It was a welcome contrast to the bickering of the rest of the crew.

Eddie also had a sixth sense when things were not right with a shot and would go to great lengths to help David's vision or in some cases the sound. It might be assumed that on a film set most of the conversation revolves around the creative endeavour. It does not. Most of that has usually been ironed out during the scripting stage and the editing department will add the final touch.

What troubles most shooting crews is food, accommodation and the annoyances that prevent the job in hand from getting completed so that they can go home. On a location picture these problems are manifold. Unpredictable weather is to be expected but there are other

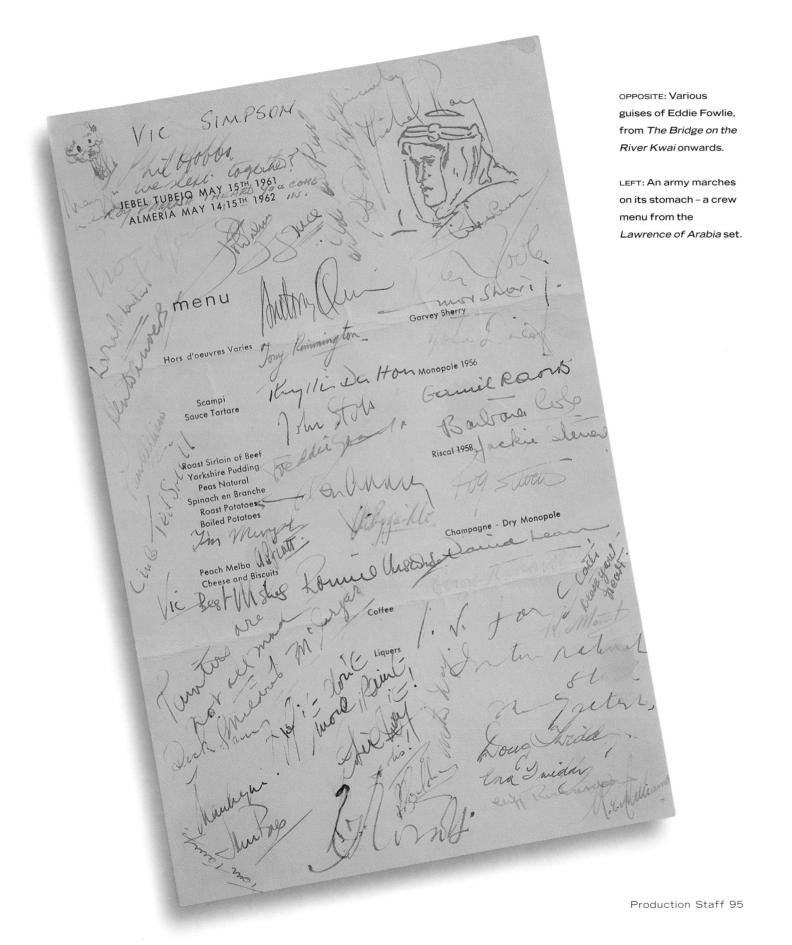

OPPOSITE: Various guises of Eddie Fowlie, from *The Bridge on the River Kwai* onwards.

LEFT: An army marches on its stomach – a crew menu from the *Lawrence of Arabia* set.

intrusions that can hold up shooting – a clear blue sky with a jet vapour trail in a period piece, for instance; or the drone of traffic when no town is supposed to be nearby and even the clucking of chickens when they should not be around.

David the raconteur would tell this story about Eddie's practical approach to problem solving. While shooting a scene in *Doctor Zhivago*, silence was of the essence. Most obeyed except for some roosters who were in a nearby farmyard. The chickens interrupted the dialogue so Eddie was summoned to subdue the offending poultry but was given strict instructions that no harm should come to the perpetrators of the noise.

After a few minutes Eddie had solved the problem and shooting continued. The chicken pests were forgotten until the next day when, preparing for the day's shooting, the crew were heard talking about the great feast they had enjoyed the night before. As it was so unusual to hear compliments instead of complaints, they were asked what the feast consisted of – "chicken" came the reply.

With suspicion Eddie was asked about how the previous day's roosters had been silenced – had they come to any harm?

Eddie looked a little shame-faced and admitted that the crew had eaten the originators of the previous day's disturbance for dinner, explaining to David, "Well, the crew were complaining about the food and you were complaining about the noise, so I thought I would kill two birds with one stone."

Eddie became David's right-hand man; he was the man who drove the train in both *The Bridge on the River Kwai* and *Lawrence of Arabia*; he was also the man who became the proud possessor of most of David's cars.

David died on April 16, 1991, when he was just about to start filming *Nostromo*. His assistant, Sarah, was adamant that I should none the less try to celebrate my birthday on May 17, so she arranged a dinner with my friends and two of David's "dedicated maniacs", Mike Stevenson and David Tringham. It was a wonderful evening; it certainly made my sadness a tad lighter and helped to lift my spirits. Having imbibed a fair quantity of red wine they started to recount many wonderful stories from their time in the Jordanian desert. They mimicked David to perfection but I could see that they held him in great esteem. Obviously they had an enormous affection for him.

ABOVE: **Cast your cares on the water – the seagull appears and the director gets his perfect shot.**

RIGHT: **John Box, who would have been art director on *Nostromo*.**

OPPOSITE: **John Box gives proportion to Venice.**

David's "dedicated maniacs".

In Memoriam (D.L.)

At the height of his power
He untangled the jungle
Uncovered the paths
That had been long forgotten
He cleared the brown bracken
Let grow the green ferns

Giving substance to dreams
We knew not existed
He extinguished a flame
To ignite the horizon
Which extended beyond
The edge of the map

No iconoclast he
He was a true romantic
He made us believe
In what lay concealed
Compassion and passion
Is what he revealed

If the embers have died
The heat they engendered
Continues to lighten
The darkness of days
It helps us endure
The void of the night

Only the weight of our sorrow
Can not be consoled.

David Tringham - May 1991

ABOVE: The poem David Tringham gave to me.

OPPOSITE: The search for the sky continues on *Nostromo*.

8 CAMERA

I love getting behind a camera and trying to get images on the screen.
DAVID LEAN

IT ALL BEGAN WITH the Box Brownie David was given at the age of eleven. He became fascinated with the pursuit of capturing the moment and the light, developing an obsession that remained part of him for the rest of his life. Who would have thought that the boy who spent all his pocket money on film and processing would one day become one of the world's leading film directors?

David believed that no one could become a film director unless they knew the art of photography.

I never understand the people who think they can direct films and they haven't learned the rudimentary principles of film-making. I would say to anyone who wanted to be a director, "Do you take photographs?" You can tell a hell of a lot from the photographs he takes. If you haven't got the eye for a camera you're in trouble if you want to be a movie director.

When Roy Stevens became his assistant director on *Lawrence of Arabia* David insisted that he take stills and that he organize a darkroom. Each Monday during pre-production Roy had to show David shots that he had enlarged and reframed. This early training with David was extremely worthwhile for the twenty-year-old Roy, as he was able to shoot some of the storm footage in *Ryan's Daughter*. He knew it had really worked when David viewed the results and said, "I don't know how the f— you did that. All I know is I wish I'd done it. Now f— off."

David rarely took photographs during the shooting of his movies but he took many while finding locations on "recces". These, very often,

became final set-ups for the production. Robert Bolt recalled that David even made him buy a small camera to use while scouting for locations.

But I would never use it when he was about. He would watch me nervously while I took my pictures and then would look away again and at last come over. "Jolly good," he would say, "but if you tilt the camera a little farther from the sun – that's it – you get a piece of Jaisal's rope. I say, would you mind shifting the other way, Jaisal. Excellent. Now, that's a fuller frame, and yet it focuses on the objects of my attention. Anyway, do you see Robert, do you see?" David sees everything, small and large, through the eyepiece of a camera and blown vigorously up into the point of view of the audience. He sees things that aren't visible to my eyes, yet they stand out in the cinema.

Although a good photographer himself, David allowed the cameramen to extend a magic to the screen. Many of the great British cameramen came from a stable that David helped to create, from Robert Krasker on *Brief Encounter* to Guy Green, Jack Hildyard and, of course, Freddie Young, whom he greatly admired.

After *Brief Encounter* Bob Krasker began shooting *Great Expectations* but David replaced him with Guy Green as he felt Bob was not delivering the contrast of light as visualized during scripting. When Bob won a cinematography Oscar for Carol Reed's *The Third*

OPPOSITE: **David freezes a Finnish lake on** *Doctor Zhivago*.

LEFT, MAIN IMAGE: "The charge
to the Chapman" on *Lawrence*.

LEFT, TOP: Freddie framing.

LEFT, BOTTOM: David with his own tracks.

ABOVE: Robert ready for
camera instructions.

Man using very strong contrasting light, David was concerned that he had been wrong. Yet the results Guy achieved ensured three more pictures with David, a grounding for his own directing career and a life-long friendship.

David knew he had to allow time for a cameraman "to paint with light." Freddie and David had a good accord.

"How long will this scene take to light?" David would ask.

"About eight hours."

"I'll come back tomorrow and see it then."

Herb Lightman, the editor of the magazine *American Cinematographer*, observed the relationship between Freddie Young and David during the shooting of *Ryan's Daughter*:

> Lean and Young appear to jog everywhere. Up and down vast stretches of beach, selecting camera angles. Their vitality is absolutely incredible, very much like that which teenagers are supposed to have. Freddie, in his red hat and socks, seems to be in eight places at once, personally checking out every detail relating to the camera.
>
> The rapport between director and cinematographer is a lovely thing to behold – two highly individualized cinema craftsmen functioning as a single creative entity. **One can finally begin to understand how *Lawrence* and *Zhivago* came into being**.

There is a school of thought that Freddie won his Oscars on David's films because he had been prevented from filming when he thought everything was satisfactory. Freddie was quick to create his lighting but David would not turn over the camera until he felt the time was perfect. "Just wait a few minutes more, then the sun will be ideal for the scene," the director would tell a waiting camera crew. It frustrated everyone but he was right.

Yet it was his obsessive perfectionism that caused most of David's trouble with the "money men". He knew each image had to be the best he could achieve and would simply wait until he got what he wanted, which infuriated production executives. He understood their problems but he had to be certain that the audience marvelled at the spectacle: great lighting, great scenes and great imagination. **"I only want to make films that I want to see,"** he would say, and this is exactly what he did.

His love of photography did have its boundaries; there were certain subjects that he felt the camera should not explore. He could not see any point in violence on the screen. His productions contained violent scenes but he preferred these to be reflected in the facial expressions of an actor, which he believed had more emotional impact. He trusted the imagination of the audience to be much stronger than any orgy of special effects.

Planning memorable scenes.

ABOVE: Sarah Miles on *Ryan's Daughter*.

LEFT: David with Sessue Hayakawa on *The Bridge on the River Kwai*.

RIGHT: David and crew on *Doctor Zhivago*.

ABOVE: The "originals" of
legendary *Lawrence* shots.

For example, the audience does not see the blood bath that Zhivago witnesses from his window, or the massacre that Lawrence observes. In both these scenes the action is simply reflected in the face of the main characters – Omar or Peter – and then the camera explores the consequence of the violence.

David used photography to enhance a story, to provide the setting and often to contrast with the obvious. It was using this technique that brought him into conflict with Nicolas Roeg, who was the original cameraman on *Doctor Zhivago*. For the scene involving the slaughter of the Cossack children, Nic assumed David would want harsh, violent light and lit the scene in that manner. David looked at the result and had to change the set-up for he wanted soft, beautiful lighting to contrast with the violence. He wanted the audience to react with horror that such a bloody act could be fought in a beautiful field of poppies.

Likewise, when Julie Christie's Lara had her liaison with Rod Steiger's Komarovsky, Nic lit the scene in the predictable soft romantic style; however, David wanted harsh contrast lighting to highlight the emotion that was felt by Lara at this enforced encounter.

Contrast within the subject matter was also a David Lean hallmark. In the opening scenes of *The Bridge on the River Kwai* the column of British Army prisoners march in perfect unison while whistling "Colonel Bogey". They are sure of stride and give the impression of

ABOVE: Waiting for the "light" on the white cliffs of Dover
during the shooting for *In Which We Serve.*

OVERLEAF: Publicity for *Ryan's Daughter.*

A story of love.
Filmed by David Lean
Ryan's Daughter

fighting troops – until the camera reveals their shoes.

The audience sees battered boots barely holding together, down-at-heel, soles flapping and without laces. In a beautifully composed shot, this battered footwear is seen through the perfectly shining high boots of the Japanese Commander as he looks down on his charges. In one assured image the plight of victor and vanquished is memorably established.

David demanded both an understanding of the techniques that can be brought to a film through photography and an excitement in the process. Although David had great success when he worked with Jack Hildyard on *Summer Madness* and *The Bridge on the River Kwai*, he never felt that Jack had the dedication he believed his crew should bring. Like so many British technicians in the 1950s, Jack gave the impression of just doing a job. That he would not stay every night to view the rushes on *Kwai* probably resulted in his not being taken on to *Lawrence* despite his Oscar for *Kwai*.

David used recurring visual imagery. His own photography repeated the image of a hand on the shoulder, which was then used to great effect in *Brief Encounter* and *Ryan's Daughter*. Trees and branches in the foreground added to the depth of shots in *Great Expectations*, *Oliver Twist* and *Doctor Zhivago*. Glasses and goggles were used to

effect – bloodied in *Zhivago* after the cavalry attack, and flung from the scene of the motorbike crash in *Lawrence*.

David stored images and scenes in his mind waiting for the occasion for their dramatic use. A letter written in 1955 from David's friend, the actor André Morrell, who appeared in *Summer Madness* and *Kwai*, details an illicit incident in a woodland. It was nearly fifteen years before the episode was brought to the screen in *Ryan's Daughter* where exactly the same circumstances as portrayed by André were reproduced as Sarah Miles made love with the British officer in a bluebell wood.

Still photography captures lighting and framing but with cinematography there is the added bonus of movement, which David used to such great effect. He was also not above borrowing shots from his favourite films. He admired Lewis Milestone's *All Quiet on the Western Front* and would use this as an example of the power of camera movement. "When the attack starts and they [the French soldiers] start coming over the top, he [Milestone] tracks along the whole length of that trench. It's a fantastic effect. You could ask him why he does that, and I suppose he would answer that he thought it would raise the dramatic intensity …"

In *Lawrence* after a train is blown up the camera tracks along the roof of the carriages, following Peter's feet while in the background the Arab fighters cheer. At the end of the train Lawrence stops and faces his force in a heavily backlit frame. The lighting adds a luminous radiance to the young Englishman that confirms his power. The shot breaks most of the then current theories of photography but proved the experimentation of the single-minded schoolboy had greatly benefited the man.

RIGHT: **Jack Hildyard takes the exposure of Katherine Hepburn,** *Summer Madness.*

CENTRE AND FAR RIGHT: **André Morell, who detailed "Love in a Bluebell Wood" in the letter above, which formed the love scene in** *Ryan's Daughter.*

Some of David's favourite
photographic shots.

9 HAIR, MAKE-UP AND COSTUME

Now, that's what a film director should look like.

AUDREY WILDER, WIFE OF DIRECTOR BILLY WILDER ON DAVID

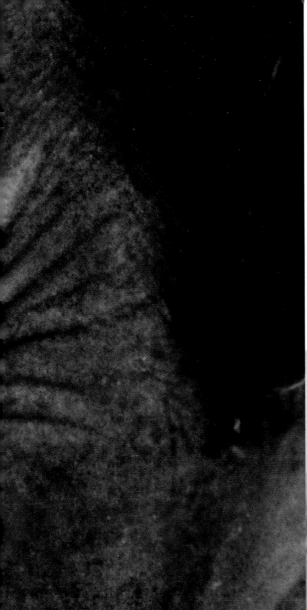

BELOW: Chief hairdresser
A. G. Scott (Scottie)
protects himself
from the elements
while doing Peter's
hair on *Lawrence*.

"MY VISION IS 20/20" David said when he was eighty. And it was – those hooded piercing eyes absorbed not only what was directly ahead, but seemed to have antennae that took in all surrounding areas. They functioned like a panning camera and somehow retained every detail immediately, taking in atmosphere and colour almost like a bird in flight. I appreciated this quality in him and learned from it and although I too have a strong visual sense, having dealt with paintings by Old Masters for many years, I could never achieve David's accuracy and focus. It was a gift, which I don't think he realized he possessed. He studied a landscape and the light for quite some time before taking a photograph to make sure that he got absolutely the right frame. His body movements were unique and graceful. He would close his right hand to form a circle and put it against his right eye likening it to a camera lens and, at the same time, tilt his head slightly backwards closing his left eye. **"You see,"** he said, **"you never get the same view through a camera lens as you do with the eye."**

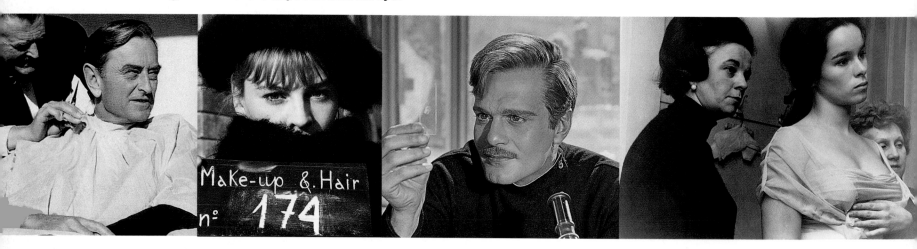

Nothing went unnoticed; the eagle-like eyes were ever alert. I would appreciate his compliments about, say, a table setting or flowers I had arranged. Always the director, David also tried to mould me; my clothes, my make up and hair. Everything formed a picture frame in his head. For example, I would be cooking in the kitchen of the Moulin (our house in France) which led on to the terrace where we lunched every day, when the sun would suddenly shift and form the perfect frame for him. He would call "Babe come out here and stand under the olive tree – lean on the tree with the left side of your face in the sun. Head a little higher, that's it. Hold it." The Leica lens would click into place; he would take about three shots in slightly different positions and the frame he had envisaged was now transferred. Perhaps, if we had time, I would have to change the pareo I was wearing as the colour was not

ABOVE: **David oversees his own and everyone else's grooming on** *Doctor Zhivago*.

OPPOSITE: **Me at the Moulin: "That's it – hold it."**

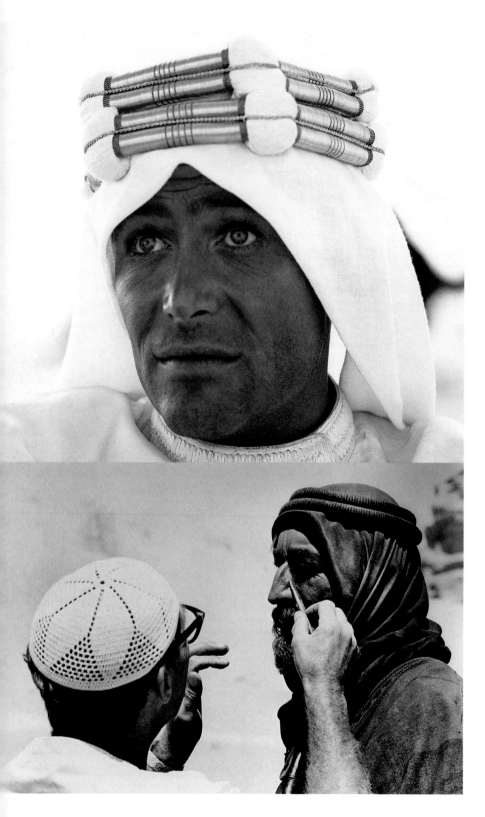

quite right, "Go and put on that wonderful shocking pink, and put something round your neck, a chain or something and hurry up."

He was "wardrobe mistress". During his early career in the studios he had worked in the wardrobe department, so it was second nature to him and – lest we forget – he was a perfectionist. In film, costume and make-up were as important to him as every other component that went into the making of a movie and so it was in his private life. He would look at me and I knew that some comment was forthcoming, "Um, black hair, black eyes, dark skin and babe, why do you always wear black – I want you to wear white." I protested and tried to persuade him against his choice. It was winter and my skin during these murky months is as murky as the weather; murky olive against white did nothing for me. "That's it, I won't go shopping with you again," he said. And he did not for quite some time. However, this ultra-sensitive mood passed and I somehow got used to his comments and eventually I found it rather pleasing that he did take an interest in my appearance. Most men would never notice if you were wearing a right shoe that was a different colour from the left. He did not much care how he himself dressed as long as he was comfortable. For days he would wear white polo-neck nylon sweaters with a navy cardigan that had "greyed" with age over a pair of silk mohair trousers that had seen better days. As I nearly always sat on the floor talking to him, I looked up one day and commented that the unpolished shoes had holes in the soles and the grim navy cardigan had a hole in the elbow. I offered to get them repaired as he was very fond of these two items. His reply could only be described as quaint, "Can you really get shoes repaired, I didn't know; I was going to throw them away!" That did it for me. I decided to try to be his "wardrobe mistress". I went about purchasing replacements. He wore clothes well and I felt proud to see him looking good. A suede jacket with a very snazzy lining became one of his favourite garments. It was often admired and he would say "come here and feel me, isn't it wonderful and look at this," as he opened the jacket to expose the lining.

When asked what his hobbies were when not directing a film he said **"I love to do nothing"** – not true because he was always collecting images in his head for the next movie. The camera was always in use.

Audrey Wilder, the wife of the director Billy Wilder, commented when seeing him in Los Angeles, "Now, that's what a film director should look like." He had been quite vain in his younger years and had a style of his own, including quite out-of-the-ordinary collarless jackets. Now, his own wardrobe was almost as interesting to him as the costumes for the characters in his films.

During the filming of *Doctor Zhivago*, Geraldine Chaplin, Charles Chaplin's daughter, who played the wife of Yuri, was filming a scene set at the railway station in Moscow. Geraldine's character was arriving

OPPOSITE, TOP: Peter wears his *bedu* robes in *Lawrence*.

OPPOSITE, BELOW: Make-up artist Charlie Parker applies the nose (to Anthony Quinn) that "launched a thousand horsemen."

RIGHT: A photograph for Issey Miyake by "Snowdon".

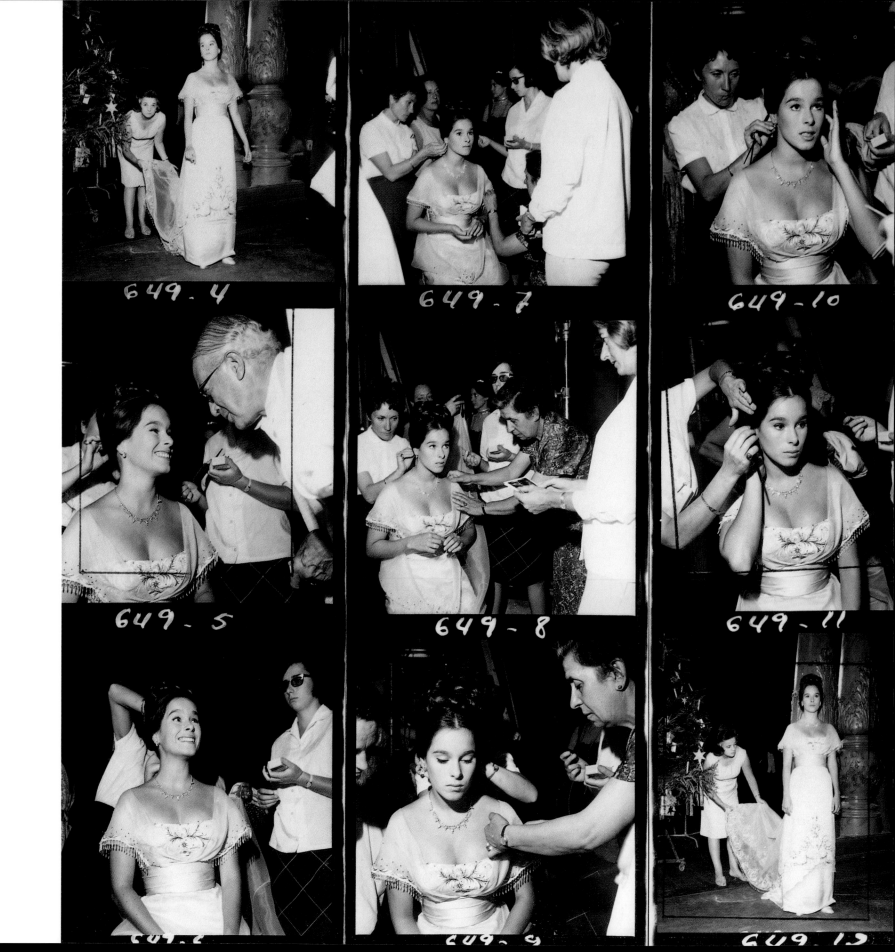

649.4

649.7

649.10

649.5

649.8

649.11

649.6

649.9

649.12

OPPOSITE AND LEFT: The crafts of make-up, hair and wardrobe are used to prepare the "belle", Geraldine Chaplin, for the ball.

BELOW: An original costume concept for *Doctor Zhivago*.

back from Paris where she had been studying. She was to wear a rather wonderful grey costume designed by Phyllis Dalton, costume designer on the film; it was a very elegant tight-fitting three-quarter-length jacket over a long, narrow skirt topped with the most beautiful hat trimmed with fur. It was to be grey as Phyllis envisaged that a costume in a pale colour would appear grimy at the end of such a long train journey. David did not take to the colour and Phyllis, feeling rather disappointed, obediently made exactly the same costume in white. It was so glamorous but David again did not approve. "Smile," he said to Geraldine. "No, no," was his answer, "it makes your teeth look yellow," and turned to Phyllis and demanded pink. **"If you do something really well on screen, an audience will always believe it is for real. If she looks great they will never question whether she's spent hours on a train or not,"** was his comment.

Phyllis resigned herself to making yet another costume. Third time lucky. He got what he wanted, Geraldine looked stunning and Phyllis was really delighted with the result. "He was right, he nearly always was," she said.

Egyptian Omar was cast as Yuri in *Doctor Zhivago*. "If we get rid of his orbs and give him a Slav-like slant to the eyes, I'm convinced they will believe he's a Russian," said David. This decided, David did not think of the discomfort that this would cause Omar. Every day the make-up department would pull his eyes into an almond shape; the skin was stretched and then taped to his temples. His hairline was then thought to be too Arab and his hair too curly. So, Omar's hairline was taken back so that his forehead was longer and slanted into his head and his hair straightened. The pain and effort must have been horrendous but was worth it because one actually believed in his characterization and that he was Russian.

far-away locations because of David's own curiosity, "It's like wandering in an ancient field," he said which came from his love of his first visit to Pompeii when he was a teenager. "It was my first experience of the ancient world. I found it terribly moving. I remember walking around in tears." These images and characters remained with him until he found an opportunity to rekindle what he had observed or read.

Interesting faces, eccentricity, flawed characters and, above all, adventure were all included in his films. Take Fagin in Charles Dickens's *Oliver Twist*: an English writer creating and an English actor bringing to life a principal character who was Jewish. Alec Guinness desperately wanted to play Fagin but David found this difficult to believe. Alec begged David to give him a film test. "Alec, with all due respect, you're mad," said David. Finally, granted a screen test, Alec appeared with full make-up. When he walked on to the set, David was stunned. "This extraordinary thing came on." Not only did he get the part but his basic look was used in the film. Alec and Stuart Freeborne, the make-up artist, did a marvellous interpretation of George Cruikshank's original drawings of the character. Slowly, we see it all coming together; the cartoon-like beaked nose, the eye-bags, the wrinkles and the beard and eyebrows made to look more authentic because they were made of real hair. It took three and a half-hours to complete Alec's make-up, changing his youthful face into that of an old man. The character of Fagin was over the top and so was his make-up. **"Alec was just wonderful,"** David told me, **"he was larger than life."**

Alec's body language and voice made the character jump out of the screen. His acting ability was extraordinary. Nobody on the set seemed to recognize Alec as Alec, they only saw Fagin. "I'll be glad to get my make-up off so I've got friends again," he said.

Oliver Twist gained accolades in Britain and Europe but was only released in America after twelve minutes that America thought to be Anti-Semitic had been cut. It was criticized as "the worst caricature of a Jew ever depicted in an English film." The famous nose had to be altered. I find this attitude strange because Alec holds the balance well and does not turn him into either a loveable Semitic rascal or a victim of anti-Semitic prejudice.

Poor Omar, headaches from his part as Yuri in *Zhivago*. Poor Omar, enveloped in black robes as Ali in *Lawrence* in 130 degrees of heat in the Arabian desert, his clothes caked with his body salt each day. What dedication – it's a wonder he never thought of changing his career.

Peter's entrance as T.E. Lawrence in *Lawrence of Arabia* was modest. At first, he was dressed in uniform as an awkward army officer; then gradually one realizes that he and the desert have become one. His army uniform changes to white *bedu* robes. As the film progresses and he becomes more ethereal, so the robes become lighter and lighter. Attention to detail was rigid on the part of director and costume designer alike.

It is also interesting to note from stills taken during the filming that David was as fastidious about his own appearance as his characters. Not that he was swathed in *bedu* robes – on the contrary – he stood out from everyone, being immaculately dressed in a bright white shirt with short sleeves.

From costume to characters – the cast. We have the Arab, the Russian, the Jew, the Englishman and the American. We are taken to

Then, there was the character of Auda Abu Tayi, an Arab, played by Anthony Quinn. The location was Wadi Rumm and the film, *Lawrence*. Make-up artist Charlie Parker had applied the famous nose to Tony's face and his make-up was complete. Long before "action" was announced, Tony decided to dress in his Arab robes and nonchalantly strode down the hill where he knew he would find David and surprise him. What he did not realize was that beneath the hill sat four or five hundred Arabs sheltering from the sun. They were huddled together. Suddenly, they spotted him on the horizon and began to chant: "Auda Abu Tayi." I suppose they thought he had come "as if out of a mirage." They fell in line and followed him to David, still chanting. who enquired what the rumpus was all about. One of his assistants suggested that it was the Arabs chanting for Abu Tayi. Suddenly, David caught sight of him and said to his assistant director, "Who the hell is that man?

"I don't know," came the reply.

"Never mind," David said. "Screw Anthony Quinn, Let's hire that guy instead!"

I can recall occasions when David's vanity was accompanied a degree of nervousness that overruled his confidence. This certainly happened on set but it also occurred in his private life. On one such occasion, he was invited to 10 Downing Street. He liked Mrs Thatcher and found her attractive. "She's really very amusing," he said "and her legs are great. She has very neat ankles."

However, beforehand, he was in the most hellish mood. It was compulsory that he should wear his decorations, the CBE and the insignia of his Knighthood. "Don't be ridiculous," he said "it isn't compulsory. She doesn't care." He was like a child stamping its foot and declined to wear them until I had to call Debrett's to convince him that this was protocol, whether he liked it or not. I noticed, as he left, that he had turned his coat collar up and clasped it beneath his chin in order to hide what indeed he should have been so proud to expose. I knew the outrage was because he was nervous and, moreover, embarrassed. Nevertheless, the episode left me feeling as if I had been pulled through a hedge backwards.

One of his worst attacks of nerves came during the trip to Los Angeles when he was awarded the American Film Institute Life Achievement Award in 1990. All looks good when you see it on screen but behind the scenes beforehand it was gruesome. The mood was doom and gloom. This was partly due to the fact that David was not feeling terribly well but also because he had not yet written his speech. He had buried his head in the sand and left it until the last minute. He did not like making speeches and the written word remained ever painful. It took him forever to write and the reason was that, of course, it had to be perfect.

Another "niggle" was his vanity. Cortisone had bloated his handsome face and this really bothered him. Nevertheless, on that evening, he looked wonderful and most distinguished. I understood how he felt; this was his big night. He had always been camera-shy and very conscious of that "eye" boring in on him. All this was the cause but the effect was a tantrum. I had to cut his hair at the last minute (I always cut his hair but usually there was more time); I had to make sure the mole on his nose was covered by the right colour of make-up and I had to ensure he had the notes of his half-finished speech safely in his pocket.

Suddenly, he decided that he had to have a new bow tie and it had to be red for some unknown reason so I was summoned to run out at the last minute to search for the perfect colour. On the way back I dreamt of relaxing in a bath with all the chores completed but it just was not to be. When I returned proudly presenting the bow tie, I noticed that his eyes were swollen.

The night before he remarked that I had a slightly darker hue to my skin. I admitted that it was out of a bottle. "Put some on me," he said, which I duly did. "What about the eyes?" he said, "I don't want white rings." I warned him that the cream sometimes made the eyes swell. He insisted. So, at the last minute, when we had very little time left and I was not yet dressed, I had to stand holding ice bags over his eyes until the swelling had receded. I dressed in five minutes.

I suppose it was his modesty, his sensitivity, his shyness, his embarrassment but so much more that made me reach out to him. He wasn't the ruthless, toffee-nosed, cold perfectionist that everyone made him out to be. He was a GREAT man and I was privileged to be with him. I was so proud of him I had to fight tears. The tantrum, the fake sun tan, the mole, the haircut were all worth it and he did turn round as we left for the ceremony, looked at me and said, **"you look like a smash cat Babe."**

OPPOSITE: **David and Geraldine on the set of** *Zhivago*: **she was perfection in pink.**

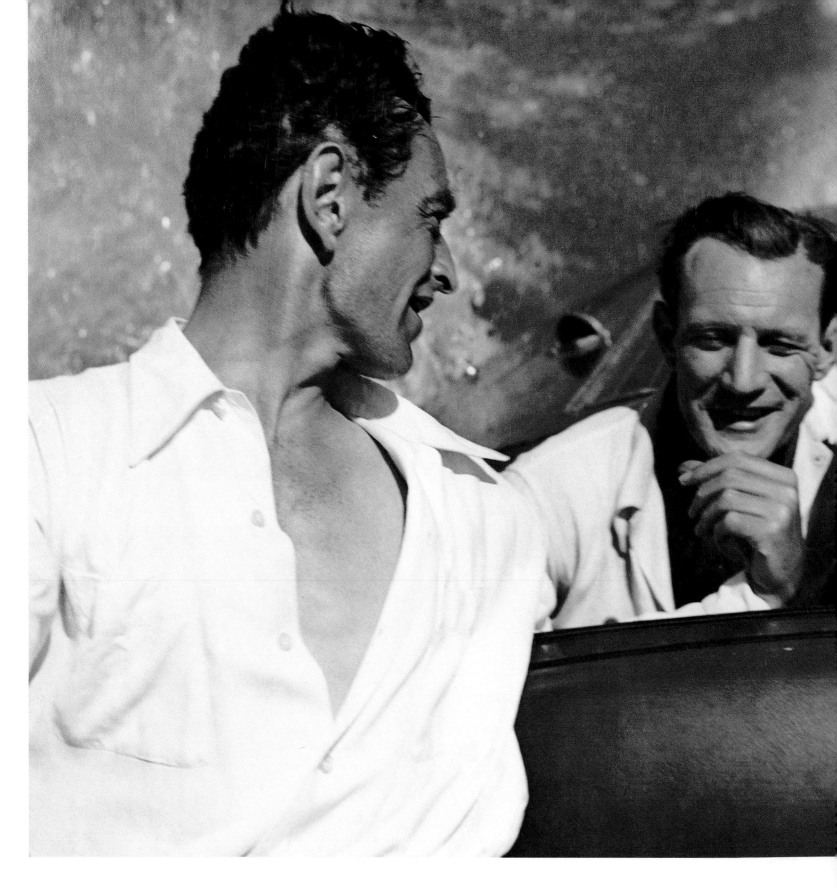

LEFT: David playing the
handsome boatman in *The
Passionate Friends* (1949), with
Trevor Howard and Ann Todd.

10 STUDIO

The awful factory dreariness
of Denham Studios.
CELIA JOHNSON

FILM STUDIOS HAD ONCE been the great escape for David. He
had swapped the confines of boring suburbia and been drawn into
these dream factories. Here craftsmen made the imagination of
writers and directors come to life before the camera. Even late in life,
after he had made the majority of his films on location, he still enjoyed
showing me around Pinewood Studios, showing me where he lived
during the war, the restaurant and the gardens. He pointed out the
massive constructions being prepared for sets, the fine work of the
plasterer's shop and the detailed work that turned a black hole of
fifteen thousand square feet into a palace or shipyard.

Most of his earlier films were made in these silent caverns where day
could become night, seas could be controlled and ghosts could
appear at will. Even *Brief Encounter* only travelled to Carnforth station
in Lancashire for establishing shots, Regent's Park for the boating lake
and Beaconsfield, in Buckinghamshire, which was just around the
corner from the huge studios at Denham. With the end of the war
location shooting became easier and *Great Expectations* spent a
month away from the "factory"; unfortunately, the unit was confined
by the script to an island in the middle of a mud flat.

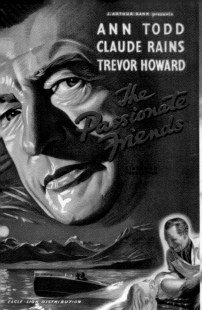

OPPOSITE: David crosses a chasm during the filming of *The Passionate Friends* in the Alps.

ABOVE: The release poster for the film.

RIGHT: David freed from the studio during the location shooting.

The Passionate Friends, which was retitled *One Woman's Story* in the U.S., afforded a trip to the Alps but with postwar financial restrictions the delights of location shooting were severely restrained. This financial constraint was not the reason for David venturing into the Hitchcock model of appearing in his own film. He only played the handsome boatman because of space considerations in the small craft.

After this break into the light David went back to the claustrophobic atmosphere of the studios. In those days, they were run very much on an industrial basis. The crews would rush home at night. They didn't share David's love of the movies. The system that existed was encouraged by the studio owners, as they wanted to make sure the crews worked efficiently. Yet some studio heads realized the problems of working in the dark spaces. Alexander Korda once said to David, **"I don't want to go into the studio again. It's like going down the mines."** And David added that he was quite right. **"Those huge doors come down and you're in a pitch-black mine. I prefer the sun."** For David, the studio restricted his horizon.

Korda gave David the opportunity to get away from the incarceration with *Summer Madness* (1955), also given a name change in the U.S., after which he was never again to make movies in a studio. This production was one of the great turning points in his life, a vast opening, to panoramas and horizons. He had a big international star in the form of Katharine Hepburn, the encouragement of Alexander Korda to shoot wide vistas, along with the ability to put a camera on top of St Mark's with the now freely available hand-held cameras from Arriflex.

Importantly, this production had the beauty of Venice as a setting for the film. David had loved Venice since discovering it in the 1930s

It Happens to **Hepburn...**

She came to Venice
a tourist
she went home
a woman !

It Happens In **Venice...**

The world's most fabulous
city as you've never
seen it — from its
web flung canals to
its colourful piazzas.

LONDON FILMS in association with LOPERT FILM PRODUCTIONS presents

KATHARINE HEPBURN
ROSSANO BRAZZI
IN DAVID LEAN'S PRODUCTION OF
Summer madness

with ISA MIRANDA

Produced by ILYA LOPERT · Directed by DAVID LEAN
Screenplay by DAVID LEAN and H.E.BATES

FILMED ON LOCATION
VENICE IN Eastman C
PRINT BY TECHNICOLE

DISTRIBUTED BY INDEPENDENT FILM DISTRIBUTORS in association with BRITISH

How the United Kingdom (ABOVE) and United States (RIGHT) released the same movie.

LEFT: Denham Studios in Buckinghamshire.

RIGHT: David's view from the top of St Mark's.

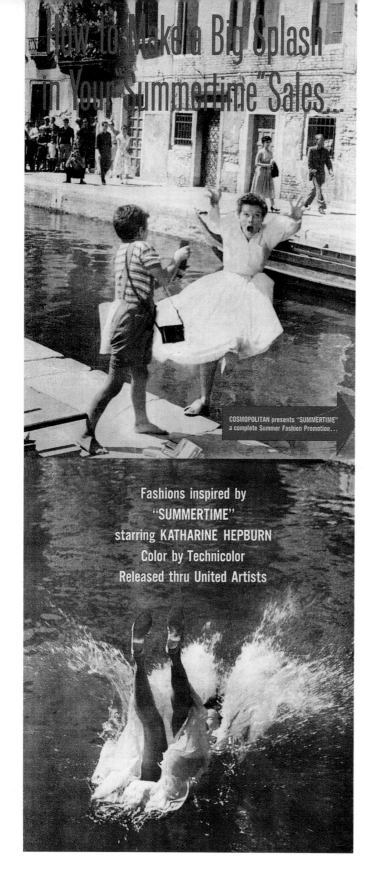

How to Make a Big Splash in Your "Summertime" Sales...

COSMOPOLITAN presents "SUMMERTIME" a complete Summer Fashion Promotion...

Fashions inspired by
"SUMMERTIME"
starring KATHARINE HEPBURN
Color by Technicolor
Released thru United Artists

while cutting *Escape Me Never* (1935), which featured the Serene Republic. He had been there before the war with a girlfriend to whom he had taught photography, but now he was returning with an important film star and an award-winning camera crew, which was a perfect antidote to the depression of London's studios, with their home-loving crews and demanding wives.

From this point on David never entirely made any production in either the studios or Britain. He preferred to make everything with a wide horizon. The journeys to locations around the world had started and one of the most productive periods in his life was on a roll. In front of him were jungles, deserts, snow-drenched fields, roaring seas and the wonders of the world. Wonderful backdrops to dramatic episodes were now the currency of the Lean eye. Had he shaken the pinched life of his early years and broken free from limited sights? Perhaps, yet he never forgot the experience these gave. He would use all his experiences now with a much larger prospect.

Summer Madness was a great benefit for David and also for Venice. The Venetian authorities felt it established them as a major stopping point for the tourist industry. In fact, many years later when I returned to Venice with David,

H.E BATES
LOVE FOR LYDIA

LEFT: Katherine Hepburn – a bigger splash in more ways than one.

ABOVE: Author H.E. Bates was co-writer on *Summer Madness* and became a lifelong friend of David's.

OPPOSITE: *Summertime* passion: Hepburn with co-star Rossano Brazzi.

as we walked in St Mark's Square, both the orchestras on either side of the square started to play the *Summer Madness* theme. A wonderful consequence for a film director to be admired by a whole city for the love he had shown for their Serene Republic – and a thrill for his escort!

David never lost his love for Venice and you would find that this most opulent of cities was never quite considered bad, even with his Quaker origins. In fact, the only time he would say that it caused him problems was when he and H. E. Bates were writing the script for *Summer Madness*, the reason being that Venice resembled a theme park on a two-week schedule. With each fresh intake of tourists the same events happened with an outstanding regularity, which started making the whole Venetian experience somewhat boring. However, until the end he never got tired of looking at these wonderful vistas with their beautiful sights.

From the dark confines of the studio David progressed through Italy and the jungle of Ceylon until he reached the ultimate vista – the desert: an unrelenting heat with no humanity for hundreds of miles, then at night a huge canopy of stars emphasizing the insignificance of

OPPOSITE: David looks down on Venice from St Mark's.

LEFT: A still from *Escape Me Never,* which David cut in the 1930s, showing the sadly missed Grand Hotel.

BOTTOM, LEFT: Tokatzian, the Venetian master developer and printer whom David used throughout his life.

TOP: Fellow "Puffers"; Noël Coward visiting the set of *Summer Madness* in Venice.

ABOVE: Me, many years later, revisiting the setting of *Summer Madness.*

even the desert itself. A great man can be made to feel modest in this setting but a modest man, like David, could feel another layer of insight. He realized that all men were unimportant in such surroundings but some could capture this isolation and bring it back to show others. Maybe, then, all could understand that the seclusion demanded singular concentration. It was here in the desert that David felt he understood himself and the part he played in the world. There were no more barriers, he realized that he could capture this vast magnificence and by doing so, give to the world a movie that has inspired so many of his fellow film-makers.

I asked Omar Sharif to recite this speech at David's memorial service at St. Paul's Cathedral in 1991:

Chapter 1, *Seven Pillars of Wisdom* T.E. Lawrence. For years we lived anyhow with one another in the naked desert, under the indifferent heaven. By day the hot sun fermented us; and we were dizzied by the beating wind. At night we were stained by dew, and shamed into pettiness by the innumerable silences of stars. We were a self-centred army without parade or gesture, devoted to freedom, the second of man's creeds, a purpose so ravenous that it devoured all our strength, a hope so transcendent that our earlier ambitions faded in its glare.

After travelling his route from narrow confines in suburban London, small cutting rooms and dark studios, David was now able to make the perfect movie. He succeeded to such an extent that Fred Zinnemann jokingly once proposed to ban David from ever directing another film because *Lawrence of Arabia* put all other directors to shame.

LEFT: **Desert home on** *Lawrence*.

RIGHT: **David's well-travelled passport.**

LEFT: **Desert home on** *Lawrence*.

RIGHT: **David's well-travelled passport.**

11 PROPERTY

I have four shirts; two suitcases and the
Rolls ... I need no other possessions
or a home.

DAVID LEAN

David is an English nomad with a
Rolls Royce and his Oscars in the
boot. He has no home, no possessions
and currently no wife.

ALEC GUINNESS

THE STORY BEGINS AT "Fairview", 38 Blenheim Crescent; in the South London suburb of Croydon. It was, until a short time ago, a ruin partly destroyed by fire with an overgrown garden and creepers growing over the front door. If David had seen this I am sure he would have incorporated it in a script. It could provide a perfect opening to one of his films. It was in fact where his life began, the home where he was born and spent his childhood.

The divorce of his parents brought about new homes and new locations and this period must have been very difficult for him. He learned to adapt. Possibly, this had much to do with his becoming a loner, a dreamer, a nomad. He coped as best as he could and controlled his feelings. Escape was inevitable. Homes from then on had little to do with their occupants. Taking holidays abroad after

REPUBLIC OF KENYA
Immigration Officer
5 DEC 1987 | 113
J.K. AIRPORT, NAIROBI

KENYA EXIT 6 FEB 1988 J.K. AIRPORT, NAIROBI

IMMIGRATION SERVICE 31 OCT 1985 (356) HONG KONG

IMMIGRATION SERVICE – 8 NOV 1985 DEPARTED (1232) HONG KONG

IMMIGRATION SERVICE 17 OCT 1985 (2079)

16 AUG 1983

LEFT: **38 Blenheim Crescent, Croydon. David's childhood home; with stamps from his passport.**

ABOVE: At home in Bora Bora,
a photograph by David.

LEFT: The sign at La Colombe d'Or,
the Provençal hotel David adored.

ABOVE: **The Gritti Palace and Grand Hotels in Venice.**

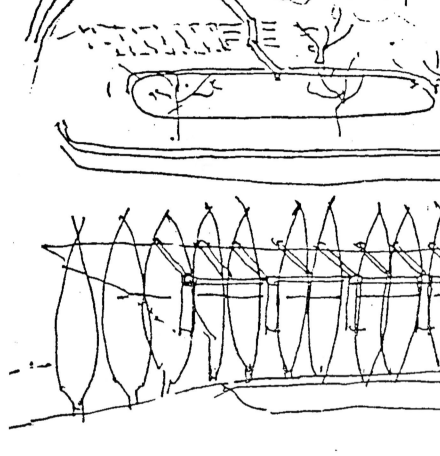

cutting a film was of paramount importance. The caravan erected upon a Mercedes truck, his home in the desert when he made *Lawrence of Arabia,* was perhaps the most memorable to him.

Now his canvas was huge and homes became hotels such as the Gritti Palace and the Grand in Venice (the latter now does not exist); the Berkeley in London; the Taj Mahal in Delhi; the Mount Kenya Safari Club at Nanyuki, Kenya and, perhaps his favourite, the Hotel Bora Bora in French Polynesia. This part of the world meant so much to him. Gauguin became one of his favourite painters, and I have many books about the artist that David collected over the years. Whenever we went to Paris, we'd spend time at museums looking at his paintings.

Observing David, one noticed that many times during the passage of a day, his head turned upwards towards the sky. He was fascinated by a cloud formation, the changing light or the floating flight movement of a bird – the eagle or seagull – which he used again and again in his films. One likened him to these phenomena. He was always on the move, searching for the perfect location, the perfect landscape, climate and light to marry with the blueprint of a story or script already in his head. His friend for thirty years, a claret-coloured 1964 convertible Rolls Royce Silver Cloud, usually accompanied him wherever he went.

There were a couple of homes on the way, which he hardly ever occupied, but these had been discarded along with the women that went with them and blocked from memory.

Together with Sandy Hotz, his fifth wife, he did buy a beautiful home just off the Appia Antica in Rome, which was designed by Stephen Grimes, the art director on *Ryan's Daughter*. In 1972 they moved in but it became a burden as he and Sandy were burgled while in the house and became scared to live there any longer. He was only to sell this home much later, after he separated from Sandy.

Towards the end of his life the nomad David, just like the eagle, came home to roost. The site was a series of warehouses named "Sun Wharf", situated in the middle of a bend on the River Thames. He had come full circle after thirty years migration and came to rest, albeit temporarily, at exactly the Dickensian landscape that had fired his imagination for *Oliver Twist* and *Great Expectations*. "I want to stretch my eyes," he said. Another strange coincidence was that Captain Bligh, who had so fascinated David, had lived just around the corner and the *Bounty* had been altered by the Admiralty just down the river.

Direction started. Action. Architects, decorators and builders were cast. There were to be four floors to the house and two terraces but no garden. The most important consideration was that of the home for the long-term claret companion. The garage was designed complete with turntable as the road outside was as narrow as its name suggested.

ABOVE: **Plans for
a Tuscan home.**

BELOW: **Summer at the
Moulin, our home in France.**

The production had long since gone over budget as interior designers
were hired and fired. One, who shall be nameless, wanted to paint the
staircase a sort of Bordeaux colour, which upset David enormously; he
loved wood so much in its natural form that one noticed him touching it
almost as he touched the skin on a woman's body. The top floor was
redesigned from a clinical white space to a warm Tuscan farmhouse
kitchen where David loved entertaining, sitting at the head of a beautiful
long table where he would enjoy telling stories about the film world.

It was strange and, at the same time, gratifying for me to see how well
he fitted into his own home and to remember something he had said
earlier in his life:

I just have four suitcases and the Rolls with a left-hand
drive. I chose a Rolls because if it were to break down in
the desert, I know they'd ship a part out right away. I
need no other possessions or a home – that would tie me

down. When I'm not working or travelling, I take a hotel room in either Venice or Rome and that is that.

One day the Eagle stood over his nest and felt disgruntled. He declared that a large garden would complete his perfect view. Twenty-year-old trees were ordered and cranes were hired to haul them from a boat on the river, over the garden wall to be placed exactly where the Eagle's eye desired. While David was filming *A Passage to India* the direction of Sun Wharf continued from Bangalore as architects were flown out, first class, for him to decide on such details as the design of a newel post for the staircase connecting all four floors.

Finally, in 1984, both productions were complete. Another was, of course, being considered, which was an adaptation of J. G. Ballard's *Empire of the Sun*. He had not yet moved into Sun Wharf but warmer climes called and he migrated in search of a location, incorporating yet another "cut" in his life. Sandy had left him. Again, he escaped from reality into celluloid and with a new lady on his arm – me – travelled for another seven months, finally deciding to discard *Empire of The Sun*. He had by this time let the dust settle and was ready to move into Sun Wharf. With this new move came a new production, *Nostromo*. With

ABOVE: **David on the terrace at Narrow Street.**

SUN
WHARF

the famous Lean–Bolt team already working on the script, recces became of prime importance and also warmth away from the grey skies of the London winter. "Hmm," he said one day, tilting the famous lion-like head upwards. There was about a three-minute pause and I wondered what the hell was going to emerge. I knew that whatever it was had been thought about a great deal and was about to be voiced. "Tomorrow, we're going to Mexico." That was it. I could never say, "can't we have a few more days so that I can organize three houses?" I just had to get up and go. We flew to Mexico the next day and recces were organized by Eddie and John and we remained there for six weeks.

When we returned, a sudden decision was made by him to relocate to the Colombe D'Or, situated in St Paul de Vence in southern Provence, to continue work on the script. During this time he fell in love with a fifteenth-century olive mill, Moulin du Jardinier, situated in the hills overlooking the Alpes Maritimes. When he saw this house, he said **"What more could I want? All I want to do is lie down in the grass and look up through the silver of the olive trees to the blue sky above."**

Another production began, this time on the mill, which took fifteen months to renovate. David's top priority was to widen the bridge over

LEFT: **Sun Wharf from the Thames before renovation.**

RIGHT: **Narrow Street, and (INSET) David's study.**

LEFT, INSET: Front door of the Moulin.

LEFT: A Bruce Church watercolour
of the summer terrace at the Moulin.

ABOVE: Interior of the Moulin.

the canal, at the entrance to the property, to accommodate his fat claret-coloured friend, his Rolls Royce. This was to be where, at last, this nomad stopped searching. He had everything he wanted, sun, the chirping of birds, butterflies, crickets and a beautiful garden with his beloved sunflowers and roses that went on blooming until the end of October. I will always remember his comment when the bush roses started to wither. He looked rather sad and said "Babe they look like yesterday's wedding bouquet!" This was the atmosphere he cherished and work came easily to him.

The Mediterranean definitely suited his temperament. His mood changed when the sun shone. I am reminded of a speech by Laura in *Brief Encounter* when she says "Do you know, I believe we should all behave quite differently if we lived in a warm, sunny climate all the time. We shouldn't be so withdrawn and shy and difficult."

He was a great host when in sync with the people around him but God help us all when he was bored. We hardly ever had to witness this as the warmth and atmosphere of the Moulin certainly prevented this from happening too often. He was in his element outside on the terrace in the Mediterranean sun entertaining his potential cast for *Nostromo* – Yves Montand, Anthony Quinn, Christophe Lambert and Isabella Rossellini were among the many who were to visit the Moulin.

Having discovered the hills in France the editor within him thought of the great director's cut. What better than the three-hour drive that linked the olive mill to an idyllic farmhouse set in the Tuscan hills above Luca? Both views were magnificent. His constant friend, Babe, the Rolls Royce would take him to and fro. Already thinking beyond *Nostromo*, he looked forward to his next film. **"I want to make one more movie, perhaps smaller this time. A love story. Before I keel. It will be wonderful to write a script in the Tuscan hills."**

Both houses had a very spiritual feeling to them – they were happy homes and one felt that the past owners had been very special people. The Italian farmhouse was totally undeveloped, and the master bedroom was simply a hayloft with a magnificent view over the Umbrian hills. The planned conversion would retain much of the original shape of the building. ACTION: ideas flowed because of the magnificence of the property.

In Italy, one needs an architect to ease the problems that a foreigner has with the Italian town planners who, thank goodness, preserve the façades of historical buildings. Our architect was rather eccentric which was a relief as it was a sign that he was probably more creative and less likely to be blinkered. He had been very ill and had found an old spiritual priest in Rome who had cleansed him but told him that thereafter he must drink lettuce juice, which he did religiously. We had designed the house and the garden. The colours of the landscape would be echoed throughout the house. It was such an exciting project for us.

Sadly, Babe never to-od and fro-od, *Nostromo* was never to be made, nor the love story. The Tuscan farmhouse was never completed. David died four weeks before the shooting of *Nostromo* should have commenced. I have scattered his ashes in the grounds of the Moulin, high above the house in the hills of Provence below the olive trees, with the blue sky above.

The waving grass, the flowers, the gnarled tree and the butterflies.

CLOSING LINES OF THE LEAN–BOLT SCRIPT OF *NOSTROMO*, JANUARY 1991

OPPOSITE: **A favourite walk in the garden of the Moulin.**

LEFT: **Déjeuner.**

ABOVE: **The traveller domiciled.**

12 ART DEPARTMENT

John's sets are all planned to be shot from one angle, it
takes away from my freedom, but they're so bloody
good I don't mind. He is not frightened to exaggerate,
to depart from reality.

DAVID LEAN ON JOHN BRYAN, ART DIRECTOR ON *GREAT EXPECTATIONS* THROUGH TO *MADELEINE*

Preparing the desert during *Lawrence of Arabia*.

THE VISUAL REALITY OF David's early productions was swiftly replaced when John Bryan, who had worked with another art director, Vincent Korda, imbued David with fresh visual excitement for *Great Expectations*. With this Dickens tale the imagination was given a fuller aspect. Good art directors on movies serve as a stepping stone for the director between script and the physical manifestation, which the camera has to capture. David always worked very closely with his art directors. The script would be fully discussed in order for the perfect sets to come about. There were no boundaries, everything had to match David's vision. **"You see, it's slightly unreal, sort of over the top but the audience believe it is real."**

Although *In Which We Serve* was mainly shot in the studio, the then biggest rig to rock a boat was constructed, creating the illusion the boat was real. From then on David carried this "real" expectation into all his films.

The famous opening sequence in *Great Expectations* was shot in a studio. For many years it was used by the British Film Institute to show how cinematic tension can be created. Even though the trees had faces and the church in the background was only five feet tall, the sequence moves the loneliness and the fear of the Thames marshes effortlessly into the minds of the audience.

When David's movies were on locations dealing with real subjects, the eye for perfectionism went beyond the needs of the camera – there was another motive, which is best voiced by John Box, the art director of *Lawrence of Arabia*, *Doctor Zhivago* and *A Passage to India*. "You

From art director John Bryan's conception (ABOVE LEFT and RIGHT) through production (ABOVE, CENTRE) – John Mills and Alec Guinness as Pip and Pocket and (ABOVE RIGHT) Anthony Wager as young Pip – to the film's release poster (LEFT).

have got to create a world in which the actors play out those parts and you have to help the actors. It does help them if you get it right."

David and John shared the same vision. They wanted everything to be realistic, even if straight after construction and filming it would be destroyed, such as happened to the city of Aqaba for *Lawrence of Arabia*. The city was painstakingly created and then Lawrence's forces smashed the city as they took the great guns, which faced the sea, unexpectedly from the desert.

This city was constructed in Spain as the whole unit had been made to leave Jordan, going first to Morocco and then to Spain at Sam Spiegel's insistence, as he feared the Arab–Israeli conflict. Thanks to the skills of the film's technicians this move is never detected in the final production.

For *Doctor Zhivago*, David and John travelled many thousands of miles looking for locations until, again, they settled on Spain as the country in which to construct the city of Moscow. Eight hundred men spent eighteen months building two perfect streets. Geraldine Chaplin recalled: "All the houses were real houses in the two streets. *Our* house was where we also shot the interiors."

Although Spain has similar weather conditions to Arabia, there is little similarity between the weather in Spain and that of Russia. The wonderful snow palace was in fact filmed in temperatures of over 100 degrees, using artificial snow mixed with marble to give the right reflection. To create the interior of the frozen palace a careful application of candle wax and water was used. The melted wax was hosed down until the perfect icicles were formed.

For *Ryan's Daughter*, the whole village had to be built in stone as David wanted it to be a village with a history – for the camera, for the actors and for the audience.

David also drew on another aspect of John's talents – unbeknown to John. When filming *A Passage to India* David wanted to give James Fox an indication of how his character should be played. He quietly told James to observe John Box and base his performance on John's mannerisms.

Although his knowledge of film location had to be exact, David never actually thought enough about where *he* wanted to live.

He had spent years of his life in hotels where the decoration followed the opulence or practicality of the management. For David, hotels were convenient as a place to work and were just stopping-off points between locations. The challenge happened when an empty "set" like our old French olive mill, the Moulin, had to be art directed so that it was fit for the modest yet successful film director.

David liked my house in South Kensington, so it seemed logical that I would convert the Moulin. Initially David thought John Box should help me. "After all," David said, "John has an architectural

LEFT: Art director John Box with "Aqaba", the city he built to be destroyed in *Lawrence of Arabia*.

Doctor Zhivago: a
snow palace in the mud.

background. You don't." Unfortunately, although it wasn't John's work, I had seen the clear cold spaces of Narrow Street with their "architectural" influence. It had magnificent views but it did not reflect any warmth or quality befitting David.

So with some trepidation on my part and some reluctance on his I persuaded David to let me have a free hand with the Moulin. Fortunately things went well, but there was the "staircase incident".

I had decided the main room in the house needed a staircase that ran down from the bedrooms and the library. It would give a great feature to the twenty-five-feet high room but it needed to run across the top of the fireplace. David and John decided I was mad but I knew it would be perfect.

During the building work, while David was in Narrow Street working on the script of *Nostromo*, I had to fit into my already busy schedule a trip to France every two weeks, each lasting a couple of days.

On one of these trips, David decided to join me. The staircase was new and unfortunately white in its raw form; it stood out like a sore thumb, contrasting with the mellowed fifteenth-century stone walls.

I had asked the builders to quickly age the staircase before our visit with a quick paint treatment. Sadly, this instruction was forgotten. David's reaction was predictable – "too grand, not in keeping with the house – John Box was right." After much ado, it was decided that I should continue to complete my vision.

A few weeks later when the house was finished David arrived and took a very measured walk alone around the house. I waited in nervous anticipation. At the end of his tour as we stood in this stunning space in front of the fireplace, he turned to me and with tears in his eyes, hugged me and said, "Babe, it's so beautiful, thank you."

It was a wonderful reaction from him – I had been able to achieve what David wanted.

LEFT: **My home in South Kensington.**
RIGHT: **The contentious staircase at the Moulin.**

MAIN PICTURE: Warner Bros. announces David's *Bounty* picture.

BOTTOM, INSET AND FAR RIGHT: David's love of the subject and the surroundings, and the discovery of the *Bounty*'s anchor while he was on location, excited his faith in the project. However, this enthusiasm ruined his friendship with John Box (BELOW) until *Passage To India*.

Warner Bros. announces
David Lean's
next film based on
"Captain Bligh and Mister Christian"
By Richard Hough.
Robert Bolt is writing the screenplay.
John Box is designing.
Phil Kellogg is producing.

Preparations are underway
in the South Seas to
start shooting in 1978.

David's need to bring visual stimulation to location sets cost him the suspension of his close friendship with John Box. David had worked with John since *Lawrence of Arabia* but during the creation of a film based on the mutiny on the *Bounty* these two dear friends fell out and were not to be reunited for many years until *A Passage to India* started production.

David had been captivated by the wide-open skies of the South Seas. He looked into this vast vista and could see how the vision of the Lean framing could add to this perfection of Nature. Unfortunately, the film was also about an event that happened in the eighteenth century, and therefore sets of villages and ships needed to be built, including a full-size *Bounty*.

John Box could only see problems. He said to David, "Just to buy a matchbox here costs four times more than anywhere else. It all has to be shipped in. How am I going to build the type of sets that you want, the realism, without all the facilities?"

"Well, what shall we do then?" asked David and John could only suggest other places that would make it easier for him. In reality, he wanted to go home and see his wife.

One day John and David were standing looking at the wide sweep of the Pacific that originally captured David's imagination. He turned to John and said, "Isn't this beautiful? Isn't this the most perfect place?" John was not looking at the view. He really wanted to go home and so was rather indifferent to the scene. David tried to force John's enthusiasm and said "Come on, don't you think this is the most beautiful place ever?" John simply said, "No."

David turned to him and said, "Are you with me on this film, or not?" John turned, walked across the beach and was off. The last thing David remembered was watching John leaving the island. John had needed an excuse to go back to London and this had now been given to him.

OPPOSITE AND ABOVE: **For *Ryan's Daughter* a complete village was built in stone.**

Unfortunately, as John passed through Los Angeles from Tahiti he stopped off and spoke to his agent. His agent wanted to know why John had walked off the picture and to cover this rift of the two old friends John said that David had gone mad and was now making the project into two films. This statement quickly spread through the film community. Combined with the overruns on *Ryan's Daughter*, this meant David was now abandoned by the Los Angeles film-making community and left without any money for his movie. John regretted this statement for many years and he felt responsible for preventing David from making a film until *A Passage to India*.

Nevertheless, David eventually forgave him and they were reunited. They went on to create more great illusions in more great locations. They were meticulously planning more huge sets for *Nostromo* when David died.

13 SOUND

Dogs bark when the elephant walks by.
JAMES FOX QUOTING DAVID
ON THE SET OF *A PASSAGE TO INDIA*

DAVID WAS STRIKINGLY HANDSOME, tall with a proud, leonine head. I often thought he resembled a Phoenician especially in profile. He had a wonderful bone structure, he was elegant and an old soul – he had been here many times before. His features were generous with an aquiline nose and piercing blue eyes, a sensual mouth and a shock of silver hair and **then there were the ears**. In profile they stretched in length from the top of the beautiful chiselled cheekbone right down to his bottom lip. I never measured them but on trips to Kenya, I would study the baby elephants' ears and came to the conclusion that they resembled David's. That's it, I thought, he has elephant ears. They also heard everything, never missing so much as a whisper.

I was always captivated by the aspect of these appendages whether in a photograph or in the flesh and they were often used in a way that seemed unique to David. There are so many stories but one will remain with me forever. We were staying at the Colombe d'Or Hotel in St Paul

OPPOSITE: **An African elephant photographed by David Lean.**

Sound 167

de Vence. It was at the period that he was coming to the end of the script of *Nostromo* and the producer, Serge Silberman; and the backers of the film came to lunch.

It was a beautiful balmy day and we were lunching on the terrace of the hotel when I saw Robert Mitchum entering with a group of friends. Fortunately, David was sitting with his back to the entrance. I breathed a sigh of relief and was pleased that he had not seen Mitchum, as the sight of "the star" would always reopen old war wounds suffered during the shooting of *Ryan's Daughter*. All went well until Bob, fuelled by good wine and encouraged by his friends, started telling tales from the movie. I shuddered, hoping that his conversation would be drowned by the laughter from our own table. Wafts of "And we waited and waited for David to find the perfect shot, the perfect cloud formation and the perfect light." His guests were very amused and the laughter at Mitchum's stories about this ridiculous director resounded over the terrace. I watched David and he seemed unaware that this was going on. My illusion was shattered as Robert's party got ready to leave. David crunched his chair against the stone, made a sudden turn and said, "Hello Bob. Made any good movies lately?" It was perfect timing as usual on David's part and the look of embarrassment on Bob's face, now even redder than it was from the wine, made the finale

OPPOSITE: Robert Mitchum eyes David with suspicion.

ABOVE: The Royal Scot, north of Carnforth.

TOP RIGHT: The Italian poster for *Brief Encounter*.

perfect. Mitchum, lost for words, gave a slight gesture of a wave and took his leave.

I think David was born with heightened senses and his hearing was certainly acutely tuned. Apparently anyone with such large ears is said to be born lucky and he certainly had a very good innings. This fascination with sound started when he was a child. He had a toy engine but it was only when his father took David and his brother Edward to Cornwall that this love of steam engines began and he would "train spot" at every opportunity.

My father took me to see the engine of the Cornish Riviera Express. I loved those steam engines and that's probably why I put them into my films. When I made *Brief Encounter*, we used Carnforth Railway Station as a location for the film. It was quite a big station and the *Royal Scot* used to go through every night at one fifteen. I used to stand on the edge of the platform shaking with excitement, holding Celia's arm as the thing roared through within six feet of us. Just wonderful.

ABOVE: Copies of *The Sound Barrier* are delivered to David.

He was acutely aware of any sound whether it pleased or displeased him. He was not a word man. The telephone, therefore, did not arouse any pleasure, partly because he suspected that the call might relate to something that he did not want to hear. Consequently, he would never personally answer it. Throughout his life he seldom used telephones. Whenever he did agree to talk, somebody else always dialled the number or answered the phone. Tony Reeves, his lawyer, tells an amusing story to illustrate this:

David's local "cafe" was the River Restaurant at the Savoy Hotel. After lunching there together we decided to walk back to the Berkeley Hotel where David was staying. On the way, he decided he wanted to tell Sandra [me] that he was on his way. In those days, there were no mobile telephones. I told him to use the telephone box. He lifted the receiver and started talking directly to Sandra and did not realize that money had to be used to operate the phone. He assumed that public telephones worked on the same principle as they did at home or in a hotel.

David himself said. "Used too often to explain emotion, dialogue belittles emotion. **Nothing is left to an audience's imagination. It's all said for you and it can border on sentimentality if you're not careful.**"

Visual rhythm in a film was important to him and he taught me to observe how he had used it in many ways to heighten drama and emotion; pointing out that this was often far more successful than dialogue. In *Brief Encounter* there are many examples of this technique. With hindsight we, the audience, realise we were unaware that dialogue was non-existent because we were totally absorbed in the story. One scene in particular stands out. He has "tickled" us with the chemistry, with the unresolved relationship of the two main characters, Celia Johnson and Trevor Howard. The scene starts to build. Suddenly she realizes she cannot go on seeing him, she cannot cope with the guilt that she is feeling about her husband and children. The pace quickens. We hear the rumble of the approaching train, the brakes grinding to a halt, the steam and then a suspenseful pause, the loud echo of her shoes as she runs down the sloped stone platform, the slam of the carriage door, the shrill whistle and the gush of steam from the engine as the train starts to pull away from the platform and, finally, the rapid rhythm of the train gathering speed. I found this spellbinding and could not wait to see what happened next.

I was listening to the radio during the time I was writing about *Brief Encounter*. The programme was reviewing a book about Princess Diana that her butler, Paul Burrell, had written. Out of the blue I heard Rachmaninov's "2nd Piano Concerto" playing. This music ran throughout the film and was, according to her butler, Diana's favourite piece of classical music. The princess has also been quoted as saying that *Brief Encounter* was one of the most romantic films ever made.

Lawrence of Arabia is well over three hours long but the dialogue is sparse, almost staccato. One famous David Lean sequence, which is shown over and over again, is the entrance of Ali (Omar Sharif) into the film. We are thrust into the atmosphere of the desert, the dust, the heat, its silence and its hugeness – one feels small sitting in the auditorium. We just about adjust and then we think we see something far away on the horizon – do we or is it our imagination? We screw up our eyes, we blink and then we hear a noise, a sort of lazy shuffling flip-flop. The sound is barely there but we are pulled into the screen, you can hear a pin drop, the tension is rising, the sound gets louder. What is it we see? What is it we hear? Is it a figure, is it a mirage, is it a camel? The indeterminable sound increases further, the vision is still blurred as slowly, very slowly, Ali comes into camera. There has been no movement from Lawrence and his guide who are watching but suddenly Tafas, the guide, makes a fast movement, runs to his camel, reaches for his gun. He has obviously recognized the figure coming out of the desert. Flip-flop, flip-flop and then a shot. One nearly jumps out of one's skin in the auditorium. What a sequence and without a word or a note of music for over three minutes. When that shot is fired its sound bounces over the desert, which enhances the emotion and drama of that whole scene rather like a symphony, which builds to a crescendo at the end of a movement.

David said of that scene from *Lawrence*: **"I originally cut this twice as long and then lost my nerve. I should have left it alone."**

ABOVE: Rachmaninov – from cinema to CD.

ABOVE: A contemporary newspaper
illustrates *Brief Encounter*.

In 1988, David made the "director's cut" of *Lawrence* in Los Angeles. I was sitting with him in the cutting room. Anne Coates, the brilliant editor who had originally worked with David editing *Lawrence* and for which she won an Oscar, was again working with him on the restoration of the film some twenty-five years later. "He was my mentor," she said.

It gave me such pleasure watching them work together; I realized then that, for David, directing and editing went hand in hand; that the two were inseparable; that, as he shot a film, he had already visualized how he would cut it. How right he was when he said that a director should really know how to edit a film. "It's an art in itself and a good editor puts the jigsaw together." This is where the rhythm of the film is worked and the storytelling is perfected. All in the silence of the cutting room, alone with the intimacy of his characters. An intimate man telling an intimate story, set against a wonderful backdrop where he would like to be. What he projected on to the screen was "intimacy on a vast scale."

Similarly, when writing and working on the script he never talked about his ideas until he felt he had perfected them. They were his secrets: " ... **it ruins the characters, the story and the intimacy and it breaks the flow to talk about it. Would you talk about our lovemaking to someone the next morning? No of course you wouldn't, I know, because it would kill it stone dead.**"

Hence the silence which continued sometimes through the entire duration of a lunch or dinner. Silence also because he was incapable of switching to another subject. "I'm not a light switch, you know – I can't switch on and off." Perhaps it went back to Quaker meetings when no conversation took place.

His insight into the unspoken subtleties of human power play was communicated through the body language and silences that he had carried through to modern movie-making after working on silent movies in the early days of his career.

He interpreted feelings that were never spoken but were immediately sensed through facial expressions. He touched us with silence. Omar who played the main character, Yuri, in *Doctor Zhivago*, tells the story of being rather worried at one stage about his part. He approached David with his problem. At the end of a day's shooting he would hear many compliments but sadly not about himself. "Wasn't Julie marvellous?"; "Rod Steiger gave a wonderful performance, don't you think?" and so on. Until Omar felt compelled to speak:

"David I don't hear one good comment about myself and I ask you if I am playing the part as you envisage it? I don't seem to have much to say and I'm being overlooked."

"Omar, you silly old goose," David said. "Listen to me, you are the observer; you take the audience with you through the story, your tortures, the politics. You are the key to the whole film. Everything is seen through your eyes. Wait and see, you'll be hailed as the hero when the film is released. Just go on as you are. You're doing a brilliant job of it. Trust me." No violence was shown and there was no dialogue when the communists marched on the streets of Moscow. David said of this scene:

I was very frightened of a scene we had in which a whole group of dragoons charge at a procession. I've seen so many horsemen charging people and the swords come out. You have close-ups of the sword being lifted and a close-up of a man with his head being split open falling down in the street, and it's bong, bong, boom – and it's a kind of bore and I got the idea of not showing any of it at all. So what I did was this. I had the dragoons charge down the street, the people start to run, little incidentals of the running such as a drum rolling down the street and at the moment that the clash came, I CUT TO a big close-up of Omar and I stayed on him hearing the yells and the cries as if off stage. I held it for quite some time and then cut back to the street and there were the bodies lying there. Thank goodness, it, I think, worked but if it hadn't, I'd have been cooked because I didn't shoot any of that sabre bashing.

OPPOSITE: **Contemplating Lara: Omar Sharif and Maurice Jarre on location for *Doctor Zhivago*.**
ABOVE: **Aftermath of the Cossack charge.**

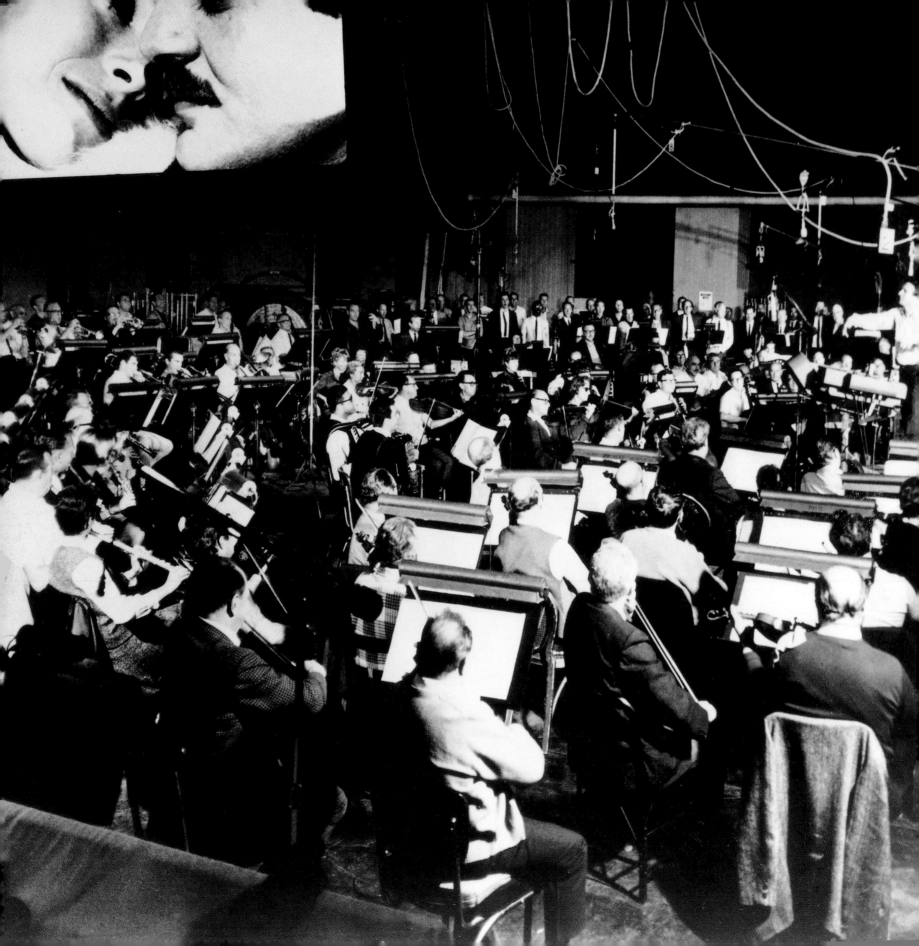

Indeed, these silences, long "David Lean pauses", body language and "eyeball to eyeball" communication were also a feature of his own life. He was adept at using them. Attention-seeking was a favourite if he felt that he was not the centre of conversation. He would fall silent and his presence became even more prominent; this continued until he had succeeded in stopping the surrounding conversation; attention then reverted to him. He had a low boredom threshold and I used to know exactly when this occurred – he would thrust his head into the air, cross his arms elegantly and look elsewhere as if observing something that had caught his eye. This was extremely off-putting. It was usually done to signify that the departure of whoever was present was well overdue and it always worked. He was so expert that he could have been an actor himself. Consequently, he did not have too much difficulty explaining exactly what he expected of them, "You see, you can express feeling without saying a word and just be still; don't gesticulate too much."

I don't remember a day passing when he did not say "listen to that." It could be in England, listening to geese flying over the Thames near the house; the roar of Concorde turning into the flight path or a ship on that same river; the trumpet cry of an elephant in Kenya, a train in India, and birds everywhere. Even simple sounds moved him; the "shush" of the shutter on his Leica camera; the muffled "clunk" as he closed the door of the Rolls, or the "clinking" of ice in his glass of whisky. These sounds would somehow be catalogued into a compartment in his head never to be forgotten and later be incorporated into a film.

I would love to write about all these sequences but I have to remember what the maestro taught me –

OPPOSITE: Mastering music for the movies.

TOP, LEFT: Peter blows us into the desert.

ABOVE: Peter relaxing with his desert companion.

LEFT: Scores for David's movies.

"always remember, be prepared to cut out your best shots." So, I have chosen but a few.

Peter O'Toole, as Lawrence, contemplates his future (as David contemplated how to cut from Cairo to the desert). David does it with no dialogue and has Peter gazing into a lit match.  As he blows the match out, with the aid of eight frames of overlapping sound, he blows on to the screen a breathtaking vista of the sun rising over the Arabian Desert. It is magical, it is emotional. Only after this does the theme music of *Lawrence* slowly rise, at the same time as we watch the slow sunrise in the desert.

Sometimes I liken David to a composer who touches us with music as David touches us with film. Like the composer, he grabs the audience within the first three minutes. Having achieved this, the music subsides a little only to increase again.

Lawrence emerges from the Sinai. We have not been bored by this long journey for one minute. The surviving boy is with him. They share a ride on the one remaining camel. Suddenly, they arrive at some sort of desolate civilization; Peter sits on the camel, nearly catatonic, his face and robes so caked with dust that he appears to have become one with the desert. This transformation seems to have sapped the last of life from him. Barbed wire leads us first to a bombed-out building. All this time the only sounds are wind, the banging of battered doors and a mere whisper of a score. The eye is led to ruins, then a screen door banging in the wind. The movement is slow and then we hear the loudest sound – the "booming" from the horn of a ship. After a beat,

BELOW: *Lawrence*: the ship in the desert.

OPPOSITE, BACKGROUND: Sheet music from the original score of *Doctor Zhivago*.

FOREGROUND: Maurice Jarre with David.

we see what they see, a ship apparently sailing through the sand dunes. They have, of course, arrived at the Suez Canal. The flow is perfect, there is no clumsiness and it is expert "cutting". It is the sound of the ship's horn that has "carried" us to the Suez Canal.

These scenes have been studied at film schools all over the world and will be written in to the history of film-making. David's peers have been quoted as saying that *Lawrence of Arabia*, *Brief Encounter* and especially *Great Expectations* and *Oliver Twist* encouraged and eventually led them into becoming film directors. In many articles, I have read these words over and over again: "There was something about his movies that made me want to tell stories." These directors would only have been teenagers when watching *Oliver Twist* and *Great Expectations*, as I was when it was shown at my school. I remember as they too remember, the pages of a book turning and a voice telling me the story: a boy running along the road, the eerie atmosphere evoked only by the creaking trees, the howling wind, then the music, a

METRO-GOLDWYN-MAYER *presents* DAVID LEAN'S FILM "DOCTOR ZHIVAGO"

Lara's Theme From "Doctor Zhivago"

By
MAURICE JARRE

Tenderly

creaking noise of the tree again, a pause as the boy puts flowers on a grave, a pause again as the boy looks at the grave; he turns to leave and sees the convict Magwitch. The boy screams. I screamed as I watched, along with the rest of my school. From here the story evolves. It scared me then and it still scares me now.

The gliding movement and shrill cry of the vulture sometimes introduced us to, or carried us away from, a location; a train chugging through the landscape would be used to stretch our eye over a vast canvas; similarly ships. Music evoked the atmosphere and the mood of the film. David would take a lot of trouble over the music and it was meticulously written into the script as the plot unfolded. Sometimes the music would be atypical as it was in *A Passage to India* or *Ryan's Daughter*; neither film has typical Indian or Irish music. I think that this came from David's fear of "bordering on sentimentality."

Jazz was his preferred music throughout his life, starting during his early teens. Ella Fitzgerald, Charlie Parker and, perhaps his favourite, Errol Garner, were especially important. He would have loved to have been a jazz pianist but sadly could not play the piano and never learned to read music. Cole Porter and Louis Armstrong were others of the chosen few. He even went as far as having a jazz pianist on the set of *Lawrence* playing the music of Errol Garner. It is extraordinary to think of *bedu* and Jordan and jazz all at the same time but that was David, the eccentric. I remember when we embarked on our first journey together to French Polynesia, we stopped off at Singapore where we bought many jazz cassettes and a Sony Walkman with small powerful speakers. The music accompanied our travels.

Strange though it may seem, David never included jazz in any of the scores for his films but the adaptations he chose perhaps did not call for such music. Success with music in his films was almost inevitable when working with the composer, Maurice Jarre. Maurice won four Oscars, with perhaps the most famous being "Lara's Theme" from the score composed for *Doctor Zhivago*. This became, and still remains, world famous. It exudes emotion. Maurice and David were very close friends and I now feel part of that friendship. Maurice tells a wonderful story about the music for *Zhivago*. David had heard a piece of Russian music but when MGM could not buy the copyright, it was over to Maurice. Of course Maurice was delighted and set to work. The first piece of music presented to David came back with a "No". "You know Maurice, I think you can do better." The second, another "No" and the third. By this time Maurice was desperate and time was against him. David decided to tell Maurice to have a weekend off and not to think about it. "Maurice, don't think about work. Don't think about music. Take your girlfriend into the mountains. You love the mountains. Don't think about Russia. Just think about love."

I don't know whether it was the girl or the mountains or both but perhaps the girl should have been christened Lara because on the Monday when he returned he sat down and composed the Lara theme in a few hours. David was thrilled this time and his parting remark to Maurice was "Perhaps you had better call the copywriters of that original piece of Russian music and tell them that I wanted to say THANK YOU!"

David's death was a deep loss to Maurice. He missed him greatly. He gave a concert at the Queen Elizabeth Hall, which was a homage to David and made a video of this concert, which he dedicated to me. This touched me more than I can say. His composition of "Offering" was a wedding present to us. He recorded this with the Los Angeles Philharmonic in 1990. We played the tape at home after we were married and I will always remember the deep feeling for David that I heard in the short sentence Maurice spoke before the music commenced. It simply said "To David and Sandra for their wedding December 1990." We included it together with music from the rest of the film scores at David's memorial service, which was held at St Paul's Cathedral, London in October 1991 with Maurice conducting the Royal Philharmonic Orchestra.

As "Lara's Theme" commenced, a shaft of sunlight beamed into the cathedral and illuminated the orchestra and Maurice. It was as if David was there, putting the finishing touches to this wonderful sound sequence. His final cut.

I walked out into the street as if I had come out of another world; this is what I remember from my youth. I thought it was my youth; it isn't, it's this great medium which has very nearly been drowned in talk. Talk has taken away some of the dreamlike quality of films as they were, and brought them down to earth. Hollywood has been called a dream factory. "Dreams that money can buy." That's one of the things I love about the movies – and it all happens in the dark.

DAVID, IN BORA BORA, APRIL 1975.

OPPOSITE: **David Bailey captures the essential David: my favourite picture of him.**

14 EDITORIAL
– SIX WIVES AND COUNTLESS OTHERS

I love cutting and editing.
DAVID LEAN

LOVE AND ROMANCE HEIGHTENED David's life and work. *Brief Encounter, Summer Madness* and the fact that David had six wives brings to mind a television interview David gave in the mid-1950s. During the programme, entitled *The Director and Film*, I was most interested to observe that the interviewer, Maureen Pryor, like most women, seemed to find him attractive and became rather coy during the discussion. She found it intriguing to discuss the romantic side of his life. She observed that in *Brief Encounter* and *Summer Madness*, "you seem to have a very great understanding of love, at any rate in one sense." She went further, mentioning love "not so much unrequited as unresolved." Faced with this question, I would have expected David's answer to be prefaced by the usual Lean pause; the "lion's" head would have tilted upwards as he thought of the right words. Instead, his reply was instant. **"That's the sixty-four thousand dollar question. Um, I like love stories, yes. I think love, if we're lucky, touches us all and it's perhaps one of the most interesting things to make a film about."** She then made a

ABOVE, FROM LEFT TO RIGHT:
David 's wives:
Isabel, Kay, Ann,
Leila, Sandy and me.

OPPOSITE: David with
Barbara Cole, with whom
he had a relationship in
the 1960s.

comment that questioned his own relationships reflected within the characters of his films. "You are more interested in a way in love that ends at its peak rather than goes on?" David's reply: **"Well, I think one's very lucky if one finds the love that does go on."**

This is perhaps the answer. David had to have a fresh excitement to drive him. He always had to find a story to fall in love with and likewise he always had to find a woman to fall in love with at the same time. This was the perfect scenario. This was the equation that gave him the energy, the oxygen rather like a drug that fuelled him.

I encouraged him to talk about his relationships because I was curious. After all his past was his present and so was mine, so why not? We would laugh about it when he told me that I was the only woman in his life who was not jealous of his "women". He questioned what had gone wrong: "That's perhaps why my relationships haven't worked. I need sexual chemistry. Um, perhaps that's not enough but neither is intelligence without sensuality." Craving affection, he was extremely tactile. He handled film in such a sensual way, as if he was caressing a woman's body; after all, the two were practically inseparable for him so it was easy to understand. He became disappointed with relationships that did not retain excitement. If they did not meet his expectations, like film, they ended up as "binned footage" on the cutting room floor. He did not waste time finding a replacement. He was always handsome and, as he aged, he gained elegance and confidence. Such was his presence that he did not need to utter a word. The buzz, the affair, had to go hand in hand with the film he was making.

Kevin Brownlow, the film historian who wrote David's biography, said to him "but David, you must have been exhausted?" "No, No," he answered. **"Energizing, energizing – an affair on a film – it makes you work even harder."**

David would not compromise either in a relationship or with technicians on a film; he was ruthless. Everything had to be as he envisaged. It was his "reel obsession" as if he was driving himself to excel.

When he was not directing a film there was nothing he liked more than to be with his lady and, with some, these became obsessive. However, when putting a film together, his obsession changed direction and film became his priority. I think this caused some jealousy and there were women in his life who could not cope with suddenly becoming "second best". I remember the first time we watched *In Which We Serve* together; as we did so I noticed at a certain point in the film tears poured unashamedly down David's face. Partly, it was because of Celia Johnson's professionalism and partly the meaning suggested between the lines to which he related. Celia played the wife of a naval officer in the film. She was talking about her enemy, her husband's ship, but if you replace the word "ship" with "film" it reminded him of what had possibly caused many of his

OPPOSITE: **With Ann during shooting of *The Passionate Friends*.**

THIS PAGE: **Ann in a Rank publicity shot.**

relationships to flounder. Here is the speech, which Celia delivered so beautifully in the film:

The most important disillusionment of all and that is wherever she goes there is always in her life an undefeated rival, her husband's ship. Whether it be a battleship or a sloop, a submarine or a destroyer, it holds first place in his heart. It comes before wife, home, children, everything. Some of us try to fight this and get badly mauled in the process, whilst others, like myself, resign themselves to the inevitable. This is what we all have to do if we want any peace of mind at all. Ladies and gentlemen, I give you my rival. It is extraordinary that anyone can be so fond and so proud of their most implacable enemy, this ship. God Bless this ship and all who sail in her.

Perhaps his first marriage to his cousin Isabel would have lasted longer if a child had not been born so early into the relationship. For David, there were too many obstacles. He had barely started a career, he did not have enough money to support himself, let alone a wife and child. There were too many holes of imperfection for the perfectionist. I am sure that Isabel was very much in love with David and Peter, his son, adores his father to this day and is very proud of him. David, however, would not compromise and could not cope with the worry and emotion of a family that early in his life. Emotion was always difficult for him to handle and film was the "great escape". When he said, "Reality is such a bore," he meant that he could not deal with reality. All his emotion went into the intimate relationships on screen instead of real life. He turned to his career, which blotted out the problems, and that became his priority. By 1932, the marriage was over for him and he simply got up and left.

David was very kind and generous to Peter and his family but that did not replace the love, recognition and affection that a son craves from his father. During the last year of his life, Maggie Unsworth (David's continuity lady on the earlier films who had remained a very close friend) and I tried hard to bring father and son together. Peter and his daughter, Tracy, came out to visit us in France. Tracy was thirty by this time and this was the first time she had met her grandfather. David was a nightmare and they left after a few days. For decades he had harboured the guilt and he did not want to be reminded of it.

There was an instant chemistry between Kay Walsh, an actress who was to become his second wife, and David when they met. They started an affair very soon afterwards. Kay remarked that she had been "struck by lightning". Most women were, including me. He was

ABOVE: "Cinema celebrities": David and Ann with Rolls Royce.

LEFT: Ann in a promotional shot for *Madeleine*.

OPPOSITE: On honeymoon at Noël Coward's Jamaican hideaway.

OPPOSITE AND INSET:
Life at sea with
fourth wife, Leila.
FAR LEFT AND CENTRE:
At their wedding with
Marlon Brando and
Barbara Hutton in
attendance.
LEFT: With Mr and
Mrs Sam Speigel.

magnetic. Falling in love instantly, Kay immediately broke off her engagement to Pownell Pellew, the ninth Viscount Exmouth.

Life was wonderful for them but then in 1937 came the slump in the film industry and from being the highest paid cutter in England, David was suddenly without a job. Somehow, he had managed to save nothing. Kay was very supportive and would do anything to lift David out of his depression but, try as she did, things started to go downhill. Of course, there were other women, but Kay was loyal and stood by him. They came and they went but David loved flattery so I suppose he thought, why not? Kay would have done anything to keep them together.

It was when he was directing *Oliver Twist* and living with Kay that David found it difficult to "marry" his obsession of film-making with his relationship. It was either one or the other. He was a man who felt he could not divide himself. He had to do everything well and his career came first. He needed help and decided to go into analysis. This quote came from David much later when he was making *Ryan's Daughter* but it could have been said earlier. It is actually David talking about David. "It is a love story and I find love pretty exciting. It is also about temptation, about the animal just beneath the skin of us all, which can be very exciting but very dangerous."

He did not like analysis, it was very hard work and he had to face up to who he really was. I talked to him about this and asked him how he had any time at all to think about himself between directing a film and a relationship. He did not answer me then but did so much later, about three months later – the longest David Lean pause of all. We were gardening together and he simply said

To answer the question you asked me some time ago about analysis, this is where I had time to think about myself, in the garden. It helped me through analysis; it is psychologically calming to dig one's hands in the earth. I had a small allotment and I just loved to go there and watch everything grow.

But, David had a dark side to him; he would project his guilt cruelly.

The woman in his life would suffer. He would purposely cause an argument; of course, the argument would have nothing to do with what had angered him but as it made him feel better, all hell ensued. Kay knew that she should leave him but that agonizing ache of love would overtake her and at the last minute she would change her mind. One day when yet another affair started, she did leave but, regretting it, left all sorts of clues lying around and David eventually found her. She was staying in the country with friends and he had walked all night from Denham, hitching lifts on the way. He certainly knew how to woo a woman and did not do anything in half measure! They were married in 1940.

He lived with women for quite a long time. Somehow, guilt caught up with him and he decided to "do the moral thing" and marry them. His timing was strange, as it would possibly be at about this juncture that most men would think of leaving their wives.

But, marriage seemed to change the relationship for David. The spontaneity disappeared. He felt trapped; there was that voice within him that cried out for freedom. So here was another "not so much unrequited but unresolved love." The marriage was finished. David wrote many years later that "Wives who are quicker-witted and more intelligent and are leaders of their family do not show their husbands to advantage."

After Kay, his attention turned to another actress, Ann Todd, whom he met on the set of his film *The Passionate Friends*. She became his third wife after his divorce from Kay in 1949. He made three films with her, *The Sound Barrier*, *Passionate Friends* and *Madeleine*. He told me later that she did not consider his needs. He felt uncomfortable with her lifestyle – a grand house in Kensington with a chauffeur-driven green Rolls Royce was not the lifestyle that he preferred. If there was one word that David could not stand to hear, it was "grand", although he liked comfort. Curiously, he was a very simple man, although what he went on to project into celluloid was on a large scale.

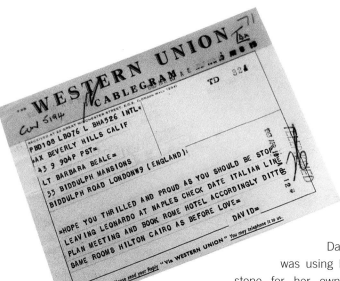

David felt that Ann was using him as a stepping stone for her own career. He was disappointed and angry. The marriage was not working out. The first thing that went was the chauffeur and, not long afterwards, the relationship itself ended. David decided that he could not continue to live with Ann. Another cut.

The marriage lasted for four years and they divorced. Ann became very bitter and a tortured period followed. For the rest of his life David would never forget the misery of this relationship and especially the break-up. He was convinced that Ann spread rumours that he was impotent, that he was homosexual and that he had abused her son. He had to leave the country, "in order to pay this woman for the harm that I was supposed to have done her. Like a fool I resisted pressures to make her the guilty party, and ran."

"I don't think you can be married to a genius. David would go away into himself every now and then. David went dead on me and he was never there. He was not marriage material," said Ann Todd.

Many years later Ann admitted that she missed the excitement that she had experienced with him. He always said that the film *Madeleine*, which was the second film he made with her, was his worst. When the marriage ended he swore never again to put an actress wife into his films.

David cut her out of his life and they did not meet again until the late 1980s. We were invited to the premiere of a film directed by John Boorman, *Hope and Glory*, which starred Sarah Miles. We were standing in the foyer of the Odeon Cinema in London's Leicester Square talking to Dick Lester, the film director, and his wife, Deidre, when I noticed a lady, possibly in her late seventies, rushing to David's side. She flung her arms around him and embraced him. They talked for a while and she left. At this point, he turned around to face me "Who the hell was that?" he enquired. I looked at Dick and there was a slight pause until I answered, "Babe, that was one of your wives!"

His expression was unforgettable. He looked stunned. "Which one, there's something in the eyes, the expression that I sort of recognize?"

"Your third wife," I said. He started to count on his fingers. We finally told him that it was Ann Todd. His reply was not surprising, as I knew that he visualized people from the past as they were then. "But she was so old," he said. When I think of it now I realize that they were about the same age, but here was this magnetic, handsome man, tall and un-stooped, appearing much younger than his years. She had aged. The film was about to start and we made our way up to the circle. I let him simmer and then he whispered to me, "Babe, take my arm – my knees are shaking."

Not just for that meeting was it was a memorable evening. As we approached our seats, David noticed Robert Bolt, whom he had not seen since they had fallen out a few years earlier. I know that David had missed Robert, missed his friendship and the close working relationship they had.

Here was another cut in his life, which he had not made any effort to resurrect. He never did. However, I felt that something had to be done to break this silence. During the interval, I tried to encourage David to approach Robert. He simply could not do it. He was afraid of being rejected and felt that it would be better left alone. I made my way over to Robert and told him that David would like to get together with him. Eventually, they did make up their differences and became friends again. I was delighted for both their sakes. I loved Robert and I could see what David had missed when they were not on speaking terms. They had a wonderful form of shorthand together.

Alexander Korda, the producer, worked closely with David on *The Sound Barrier*, which starred Ann Todd. He was aware that their relationship was in trouble but, saying nothing about this, he suggested that David should travel to India to make a film about the Taj Mahal.

THE SHOREHAM — WASHINGTON, D.C.

Feb. 24th 63.
Washington.

Baby dearest,

Thank you so very much for your 3 Singapore letters which I collected at American Express. You didn't say very how Asia was late which I was longing to hear. Now my darling L. has you and I don't want to quite leave a chance — non-romantic — I'd you more than ya

We leave in 1 or 2 days I go to L Steve is an award + (Golden Globe award hopefuls) which I'm will probably come dear I don't know — as the Academy Aw 6th (or perhaps 8th) you to remember is she must go to I (ERIC TUDOR by the in the book) She u her sister in hand she goes by boat baggage. Now. She might leave round about the middle of April

GRAND HOTEL
VENEZIA

June 19th. '63.

My darling Barbara,

One of the letters I hate because there is so little time. L. has gone out to have a coffee with an American couple and I don't quite know when the return will be. Thank you so much for the three letters at the Am. Ex. They cheered me up no end as since Robert left yesterday I've been rather depressed. Nothing terrible cropped up and no hint about us. Just that she says I am so obviously bored. It's very difficult as we seem to have so little in common these days. Had a dreadful night last night as we had one of our periodic rows with tears and all the rest of it. All started because I am an idiot and haven't yet learnt to hold my tongue when I don't agree on some issue. Started yesterday with the business about Quinn and Yolanda in the papers and L. said she probably forced him into that position and it was a sort of blackmail "like all this sort of girl". I snapped back as I can't bare this sort of moral high horse stuff which I also think is cruel and ungenerous. By the evening we were in full flight about my sins of ommission - which I know very well. Better today but it always leaves a hangover as far as I'm concerned.

First. If you really want to work you must of course do so but I do beg of you not to do it for the guilt reasons you give. What, my dear girl, would I do with my money? Keep it in the bank so that when I die it can go to some distant relative for whom I don't give a damn? This is my pleasure to spend it on you - and only such a tiny bit of it. It's a very selfish pleasure and if you want to work because you want to do some work - fine - but don't do so because you think it would be better for me to leave it to a cats home when I am dead and gone and no use to you. This may be one of your mood phases. If it is please recognise it as such and lay off further enquiries.

I was so pleased with your letters and read them out in the Piazza San Marco. Sorry about your Mum. Very trying indeed. Your hair sounds a lovely bit of heaven for me to look forward to. You must always remember I'm a conservative old thing and my first reaction is always

It was on this first visit to India in 1954 that he met Leila Devi. At the time, she was married to an Indian Civil Servant and had become Leila Matkar. David was immediately struck by the exotic looks of this woman, her posture, her beautiful saris and her outward calm. He told her she was the "spirit of the Taj Mahal". Sadly, she was a depressive and suffered greatly. David, however, thought that his love and affection were all she needed to become well again. He left India on a high note to return to Europe where he was to direct *Summer Madness*. He could not know then that this relationship was to be a constant worry to him for many years to come.

Katharine Hepburn, with whom David worked on *Summer Madness*, was to become perhaps his closest friend for the rest of his life. She understood David the man and David the film-maker.

David is sweet – simple and straight – and strong and savage; and he is the best movie director in the world. And nothing – did you hear me –

I said nothing gets in his way. He'll stand and look and stare. He won't be hurried. He won't budge until he can smell perfection. That's his aim, work or play; do it as well as it can possibly be done. Or, don't do it. For an actress, this has its advantages. You get a pure point of view. I'm not prejudiced about his direction. I see what I see, and I don't just see it through rose-coloured glasses. But, he's far superior to most people.

I could not understand why he never had an affair with her. Possibly, it was because of his enormous respect for her and an affair would have put their friendship at risk. And, of course, there was Spencer Tracy whom Kate will love until she dies. She has known most of the women in David's life and I remember what she said when David told her about us, **"Well David, if you don't marry her, I'll just have to come right over there and marry you myself."**

While he was in Venice he met Barbara Hutton, the "Woolworth Heiress" a friend of Leila who herself had gone through several

We were all privileged to visit David's favourite corners of the world – the Taj Mahal, Agra and Bora Bora, in French Polynesia.

husbands. During an evening at Barbara's home, friends teased them about their many relationships and David's comment made them all roar with laughter: **"Never mind, we're the moral ones; we marry them."**

Now, in search of the perfect love story to film, he read *The Wind Cannot Read* by Richard Mason. He returned to India thinking that perhaps a film from the book could be made there. Leila had further depression and was undergoing electric shock treatment. Her illness had made David, too, depressed. He had enough baggage of his own without this. He was miserable but still determined to get her well again. *The Wind Cannot Read* was not to be directed by David. He had made up his mind to make another film, *The Bridge on the River Kwai*, in Ceylon.

Leila's depression worsened, partly because of the women who surrounded them and partly because of David's affairs. At one point, he had Leila at the Mount Lavinia Hotel, another woman at the Galle Face Hotel and a third in Kandy. It was like a game of musical chairs. But the energizing affair had to be part of his film. Sam Spiegel, who produced *Kwai*, did not want David distracted by Leila's problem and subsequently lied to her, telling her that David did not want to see her. An exchange of letters went backwards and forwards. David was angry. He received a telegram from Leila saying "David, I never want to see you again." Again, guilt had got the better of him and he made up his mind to try to make their relationship work, but Sam continued to make things impossible and the distance between the two of them made matters even worse. David did his best and Leila finally came to Ceylon but the going was tough. Despite Leila's knowledge of David's wanderings, they finally married in 1960. Barbara Hutton organized a small wedding in Paris. The reception was at The Ritz Hotel and only close friends were invited, including Marlon Brando. Leila had risked her reputation. In India, at that time, divorce was almost unheard of, but she had also deserted her children and left India.

After the enormous success of *Kwai* David's taste for the exotic landscape was heightened and he turned his head towards the desert and Arabia. He was to direct *Lawrence of Arabia*.

Maggie Unsworth could not be with David to do continuity on the film. She had married Geoff Unsworth, the brilliant cinematographer, and had a young family to take care of. This left a big gap. The two had become close friends and David valued her advice. They were almost like brother and sister.

A new continuity lady was engaged. This was Barbara Cole who also became the new affair in his life three weeks after filming had started. At the age of fifty-three David remained irresistible to women. Soon she had moved into his "home" – I say home, it was a caravan mounted on top of a Mercedes truck. Barbara was handsome, strong and level-headed and David respected her professionalism as well as being sexually attracted to her. He used to call her his "English love" out there at Jebel Tubeiq. She was such a contrast to the troubled and exotic Leila and that must have been a great relief to him. They also had a lot in common. Barbara, of course, understood the film world and subsequently also understood David's obsession. However, it was Leila, not Barbara, who attended all public functions with David and it was Leila who accompanied him on all the publicity tours to promote the film. Barbara had been dispatched elsewhere and David, in his possessiveness, would not let her take another job on any other film.

During this time, he remained in Hollywood for four months and his nights would be consumed by writing letters to Barbara. He missed her dreadfully. These letters oozed sexuality and when I visualize this scene, it evokes *Doctor Zhivago* when Yuri's nights would be consumed by writing poetry to Lara. Barbara kept most of these letters and, on David's death, she donated them to Reading University. They were neatly typed and only interrupted if Leila made an appearance after which they continued into the night. **"It's such a lovely gift for both of us to see each other with all the façades down. It is only to you I will hand my secrets."**

In her own mind, she probably thought that their love would only last until filming ended on *Lawrence* and did not delude herself. But, David could not bear to be without her and she allowed herself to be persuaded to accept the job of continuity lady on *Zhivago* and so their affair continued.

Guilt caused him to join Leila in India where he remained for three months. Afterwards, he joined Barbara in Spain. She was building a home for them both on land that David had acquired at Carboneros near the "Aqaba" location of *Lawrence*.

In 1966, David left Spain for the Far East and India on a holiday-cum-promotional trip for *Doctor Zhivago*. The film had been an enormous success. "I realize this success was not only due to Robert and myself but also to the crew. It has made an enormous amount of money so I thought they deserved some of it too," he told me later. He sent cheques to those who had worked closely with him as a token of his thanks. In India he stayed at Laurie's Hotel in Agra where a tall blonde girl of about twenty showed David to his room.

Returning to Delhi, he wrote to Barbara describing the horrors of his marriage to Leila but said "I have adopted some sort of attitude to save myself from an involvement, which would have drowned me too. I suppose I react badly as tears are pointing a finger to one's own guilt." He started to have nightmares about her in which her softness had become venomous and she became a snake coiled around his neck. He thought it would be better for her if he left her. Leila used to lock herself away in a darkened room spending most of the day in bed. I suppose it was a plea for help but it did not seem to work. Her depression became worse.

David returned to Laurie's Hotel and did not go with Leila to Bombay where she was having further treatment "and that", he said "is when it all started." The tall blonde with the green eyes was born in India of dual nationality, Swiss and English. A fresh excitement started to stir within him.

He had only recently written to Barbara telling her how much he appreciated them being together and telling her how he did not understand her selflessness as opposed to his selfishness. Now, he wrote to tell her that it was all over. "I have fallen in love with a young girl. In my bloody arrogance I used to say I could never understand such a thing, that I was immune, above the common crowd."

The tall blonde was Sandy Hotz, whose family had been involved in the hotel business for many years in India. David's final words to Barbara were, "I am not at war with you and I pray to God that you are not at war with me. Forgive me if you can this terrible mess." Indeed, what a mess and what a quadrangle, but I suppose David was right when he said that fate leads us, and that people are put in our path to try us. I do admire dignity and Barbara certainly showed dignity, which must have been damned hard for her. She replied to this letter very simply "wishing you both well". I find that admirable.

So another cut and another chapter in his life commences with yet another girl who was swept off her feet and with a man thirty-seven years her senior. He had reached the sexual peak in his relationship with Barbara and left.

Sandy was to spend practically the next two decades with David, during twelve of which he was still married to Leila; he was frightened by her suicide threats. During those years together he made

POST ☰ OFFICE
TELEGRAM

Charges to pay
s.   d.
RECEIVED

No.   OFFICE STAMP   67

Prefix. Time handed in. Office of Origin and Service Instructions. Words.

NEWYORK 12 26 1244P

At
From
By

m

60 AL VIA COMMERCIAL CABLES J124/MG 17

COLE 33 BIDDULPH MANSIONS BIDDULPH RD LDNW9

WONDERFUL FLIGHT LOVE YOU DEE+++

COL: 33 LDNW9   4

By

B or C

For free repetition of doubtful words telephone "TELEGRAMS ENQUIRY" or call, with this form
at office of delivery. Other enquiries should be accompanied by this form, and, if possible, the envelope.

INSET:
Another of
his cables to
Barbara.

LEFT: "Great
shot babe
– hold it."
Me in India.

LEFT: "Smas
cats" on
the town.

Ryan's Daughter, which was adapted to the screen by Robert Bolt. It told a story about a young Irish woman (played by Sarah Miles, Robert's wife) who falls in love and marries a dull schoolteacher (Robert Bolt's occupation before joining the film industry). She has an affair with a shell-shocked young British officer. In a way, it paralleled David and Robert's lives, in its theme of the jealous passion for a young woman.

The girl, Ryan's daughter, rather reminded David of a conversation he had with an Indian friend of his:

We were talking about romantic or arranged marriages and he was a very intelligent, very modern-minded man and he said something which made me say to him, "Tell me, Krishna, what side do you come down on?" and he said, "I think I come down on the side of arranged marriage, if anything." I said, "Why?" He said, "Because with a romantic marriage you expect heaven. Heaven does not exist, so therefore you are bound for disappointment, while in an arranged marriage you expect nothing and if you get something you think you are extremely lucky."

After *Ryan's Daughter* David was shell shocked and bruised after being attacked by the critics and simply went into hiding. Sandy and he travelled the world and for a few years lived in Tahiti where David worked on the *Bounty* project which, sadly, never got made. He then went on to write the script and direct *A Passage to India*, adapted from the novel by E.M. Forster. In 1981, David married Sandy, but this marriage proved to be the shortest, at least on paper.

They had bought four derelict warehouses at Limehouse in the East End of London, which would be converted into a home. David told me that Sandy found this daunting because she had not experienced anything remotely on this scale. Although they had acquired a home in Rome, an interior decorator had done most of the work. They were living at the Berkeley Hotel in London during the conversion. David had accepted a knighthood and had come full circle after some thirty years in exile. Back in London, life was very difficult for Sandy. It was so different from that which she had lived during the shooting of *A Passage to India*. She enjoyed being on location. Now she was miserable. David and she no longer had much in common. They dined at the Berkeley every evening, sometimes in silence. Sandy would go about her life during the day, meeting with the decorator and architect.

David would walk to Harrod's as he loved to spend time in the bookshop. He would also visit the fish department as he appreciated their display of unusual fresh fish. These brightly coloured creatures arrived daily from all corners of the world, and I suppose they reminded him of Tahiti. He could stand there for some time just admiring the design and colour. He would finally visit the vegetable department to buy his favourite muscatel grapes and return to the Berkeley Hotel.

And this is where I enter his life. I have shopped in the food department at Harrod's since coming to live in London some thirty years ago. It was near my home and when I worked as an art dealer in St James's it was convenient for me. Cooking is one of my passions and the quality of food there is of a high standard and ingredients I needed were easily obtained here. It is odd that when anything major happens in my life, I remember details that I would otherwise not recollect. I remember, to this day, what I was wearing. It was winter, 1985.

As I was choosing my vegetables, I glanced across the food hall and noticed someone who stood out from the crowd of usual shoppers. That man has a leonine head, I thought. One of the assistants who has known me for years caught me gazing, "Do you recognize him?" he said. I felt almost embarrassed and answered that I did not. "That's David Lean, the film director," he said. "He visits about once a week and only purchases muscatel grapes." I immediately visualized scenes from his films, remembering Peter O'Toole and Omar Sharif but wondered why one never recognizes the director.

My thoughts returned to cooking and I continued to tick off my shopping list and went on my way. About ten minutes later, on my way out of the store, I bumped into him again. Without thinking – and I say without thinking – because if I had, I would never have taken the next step; I approached him and, apologizing for interrupting his privacy, I congratulated him on his tremendous achievements. He seemed happy for the conversation to continue. I thought he was charming, gracious and he seemed to be almost embarrassed at my praise. I remember noticing a sensitivity in him and it was refreshing that he was not at all pompous. We parted. I would never have seen him again had it not been for the unexpected events that followed.

My friend, Tessa, was staying with me working on a book that she was writing. Her cousin, Diccon Swan, had telephoned to say that he was coming over to see her that morning. Cut to two days earlier when Tessa and I went to see a medium who told me that I was to have a karmic relationship with a man whose name started with the letters "Da" or "Do". I had not thought about this medium since but I happened to mention him during Diccon's visit. I then went on to tell them how I had bumped into David Lean in Harrods. I was bumbling on when I noticed Diccon's expression change and his face become pale. There was a long pause. "This is weird," he said. He told us about his friendship with Sarah Lean, David's niece, and that he saw a lot of David and Sandy. He then told us that he had been to see the same medium with Sandy some two days before; furthermore that he was dining with the Leans that evening at the Berkeley Hotel. Tessa and I were aghast; it was almost unbelievable. I asked Diccon not to mention my meeting with David and he promised he would not.

Diccon called me early the next morning. "I had to break my promise to you," he said. Apparently, during dinner, David seemed pensive and the "Lean silence" was acutely evident. Finally, Diccon enquired if David was feeling all right. To this, a slight nod. After a while, he touched Diccon's arm and discreetly told him that he had met an "oriental" girl that morning who had congratulated him on his work. "I can't stop thinking about her. I will never see her again," he said. When Diccon told him of our meeting and that I was living around the corner, David was astonished and happy at the same time. Diccon finally persuaded me to cook dinner for David and Sandy and so we were formally introduced.

Life was miserable for David. Every evening, after yet another silent dinner at the Berkeley, he would arrive on my doorstep sometimes announced and sometimes unannounced. I was falling in love and realized that this was not easy. David was some thirty years my senior – a fact that didn't matter to me at all. However, I was fighting with myself. I had vowed never to get involved with a married man. Just as I was on the verge of making the painful decision to end the relationship, David announced that he had known for some considerable time that there was another waiting in "the wings" for Sandy. Naturally, that changed things for me. Life went on as before but David spent more and more time with me.

Our preferred hideaway restaurant was Daphne's, which in the early 1980s was not as it is today, large, busy and attended by many famous people. Rather, it was small, discreet and gently theatrical. David was unnoticed except by the staff. I was surprised when he ordered a double Johnny Walker in a large glass, no ice and a bottle of Perrier water, which he continued to drink throughout dinner, diluting it until he had practically drained the bottle of water. I took my time to gently persuade him to drink wine with food. He then became very interested in wines, especially claret, and wondered how he had ever imbibed so much whisky, which he had not noticed drowned the flavour of food. From time to time when he was depressed – his expression was "piano" – and he would order a "Bomba Atomica", which was a dry martini. "This will do the trick," he said. I have strong memories of these dinners. They were wonderful and painful at the same time.

Meals and walks in the park became more frequent but I would not let myself think ahead. We never discussed the subject and just enjoyed being with one another; I took it day by day. The time came that David arrived on my doorstep very early one morning and told me that Sandy was going to leave him. This was a real turning point in David's life. He had always been the one to "cut" his relationships but for the first time someone had left him. I think, deep down within him,

he knew their relationship could not last for much longer and the break would inevitably have happened with or without me. Sandy and David were divorced six weeks later.

David and I left for a six-week holiday. We finally returned to England six months later. On arrival at Heathrow, he disappeared for at least half an hour. I sat on top of a suitcase wondering where on earth he had gone. He reappeared holding a huge bouquet of flowers with three assistants behind him carrying more. All he said was "You've been bunched, welcome home." He'd bought every flower in the shop. This is a memory I will always cherish. He asked me to give up my career to be with him and so we started our life together. I was only apart from him for short periods when absolutely necessary and only thought of rushing back to be with him.

He asked me to marry him in 1990. I was so happy. He had survived the turmoils of getting *Nostromo* to the point when filming was about to start but this had put him under enormous stress. He found the problems with producers and studios tedious. At the same time he had become unwell. I realized then that life without film was not life for him. It was torture for me to see him suffer so much at the end of his life but I knew I had to be brave for him; to endeavour to smile and not show him how upset I was. I tried to encourage him and remember saying, "Babe, come on, you're a living legend and you should be so proud of yourself." He looked up at me and nudged my nose with his saying, "Babe, that is so sweet of you but, you know something, I'm a near miss." I wish that God had allowed him to survive to direct *Nostromo* but it was not to be.

The seven years I had with him were wonderful. He had black holes and black moods and he was cantankerous but he was my soulmate. He was kind, modest, generous, intelligent and had a wonderful sense of humour. I loved him deeply and I respected him. I had sunshine and I am very proud to have his name. For years after his death I felt that my right arm had been severed. I wish we could have been together forever. It was all too brief an encounter. THIS WAS HIS FINAL CUT.

To sum up to this chapter, I am reminded of a very special evening we spent in Paris with Fred Zinnemann. The three of us had dinner and ended the evening in our suite at the Lancaster Hotel. Fred and David decided to have a nightcap and started to reminisce. The conversation revolved around the women in their lives stopping only at one point, when they asked me if I objected to this private "men's" conversation. By this time we were well into the early hours, the whisky bottle was nearly empty. Suddenly they paused and Fred said in his inimitable sexy Austrian accent "The difference between you and me David is that you married your mistresses." I wish I could have taped that conversation but at the time it was just another enjoyable evening and I thought there would be many more. How wrong I was.

The perfect photographer
at work on vacation in the
South Seas.

DECEMBER 31, 1984 $1.95

TIME

AN OLD MASTER'S NEW TRIUMPH

David Lean Directs "A Passage to India"

RIGHT: The American Film Institute's Lifetime Achievement Award, presented to David in March 1990.

ABOVE: *Time* magazine salutes David's return.

OPPOSITE: Developing *A Passage to India*: David at 74, the "mountain goat".

THE AMERICAN FILM INSTITUTE EIGHTEENTH ANNUAL AWARD FOR LIFE ACHIEVEMENT IN MOTION PICTURES AND TELEVISION SIR DAVID LEAN 1990

15 POST PRODUCTION

Poor David Lean. *Lawrence of Arabia* came out and they called it "The Four Pillars of Boredom." They wee-wee'd all over it. Then *Doctor Zhivago* comes out and they say, "Oh, what a shame! *Doctor Zhivago* isn't as good as *Lawrence of Arabia*. David Lean has lost his touch." Then he does *Ryan's Daughter*. They wee-wee'd all over it and say, "He'll never do another *Zhivago*."

SARAH MILES

CRITICS CIRCLE, ALGONQUIN HOTEL, NEW YORK, 1970
"Can you please explain how the man that directed *Brief Encounter* could have directed this piece of bullshit you call *Ryan's Daughter*?"

This remark came from the infamous interview with David and the Critics Circle in New York. This was the meeting at which Pauline Kael and Richard Schickel destroyed him. David hibernated in his shell for nearly fourteen years harbouring their onslaught, after making *Ryan's Daughter*. He did not direct another movie until his adaptation of E.M. Forster's *A Passage to India* in 1984.

He was always wary of the critics throughout his movie-making life but this interview completely devastated him and he was too British to "give as good as he got." If only critics would try to be a little more sensitive but I suppose that's why they are critics. However, it is pointless rambling on about them; but they delivered "below the belt" remarks that slashed David's confidence so hard that he exiled himself from film, almost like grieving a death. There was an aborted attempt to make the *Bounty* film in Tahiti and *Gandhi* in India but David had lost his nerve and feared that his script for *Gandhi* was not good enough. Richard Attenborough heard that David was not going

to make the film and asked him if he could take it over. The film was finally released in 1982 and won Richard an Academy Award. I was recently talking to Don Ashton, production designer on *The Bridge on the River Kwai* and of course he was reminiscing. The subject of *Gandhi* came up and I said what a great film David could have made. It was sad that he never got round to directing it. Don gave me a long look and said, "It's a good job he didn't, he'd probably still be doing it!" There were other scripts that were brought to his attention but nothing seemed to "fire" him. Nobody seemed to be able to get him back up on that horse again until *A Passage to India*.

At last, his hibernation was at an end. He slowly emerged from his shell with utmost caution; he felt insecure and, with such Oscar-winning films as *The Bridge on the River Kwai* and *Lawrence of Arabia* to his name, now more then ever, he had to come up with something as big or bigger. This after all was his resurrection and the restoration of his career.

David felt an empathy with Forster; like David, Forster fought against his suburban childhood and like David, Forster loved India, where he made two lengthy stays, learning to know India and loathe imperialism. David felt compassion for the people and a passion for the nation. "You either love it or hate it, there's no grey area," he said.

Recce shots for
A Passage to India.

I've often wondered why Europeans first arriving in the East either like or hate it. Lids tend to come off. Some become deeply disturbed. It may be that India somehow reflects echoes of our distant past where our inhabitants weren't so strong. In a sense we do walk down our aircraft steps into the past.

Forster had continually denied anyone the film rights to his novel but had allowed Santha Rama Rau to adapt it into a stage production, which David had seen. Even Anthony Havelock-Allan, who was a friend of Santha Rau's family, was refused permission. Finally, Lord Brabourne, whose father-in-law, Earl Mountbatten of Burma, had been the last Viceroy of India, acquired the rights and approached David to direct the film. It was not without problems. Forster had stipulated in his will that only Santha Rama should write the film script. David found her difficult and felt that her script would not adapt to the screen; it was embarrassing for him to explain his frustrations to someone who had never written a film script. In a letter to Santha Rama Rau, he talked about film-making,

I often think of a film as a train journey. The permanent way, the rails, are the story line. Very soon, after the titles the train gathers speed and reaches its narrative cruising speed. Tickity-tat, tickity-tat. Woe betide us

RIGHT AND OPPOSITE:

David was captivated
by Kashmir and
incorporated it into
A Passage into India.

with that impatient audience if we slow down to examine an interesting detail of the passing landscape. They'll open the popcorn, kiss their girlfriend and light up a cigarette. We'll have to show them those details while we're still travelling or it'll take an earthquake or an elephant charge to regain their attention.

That said it all. Her script was too literary and not at all suitable for the screen and it was one that I suppose David inwardly sensed would have harmed his reputation. He always wanted to write the script and finally John Brabourne suggested that he should. His "voice" suddenly became strong when he announced that he wanted sole credit. He had written several scripts in collaboration with Robert Bolt and earlier scripts during the time of Cineguild. He had never taken any credit, "so why shouldn't I get credit on this one? I want to write a script and make a movie which is true to the book but which will also appeal to the man in the street."

His understanding of India, the people and their philosophy certainly came into his script; his description of Mrs Moore "an old soul who has been here many times before." This was David speaking as I remember him thus describing people; the philosophy of the Wheel of Life: "it has many spokes, a continuous cycle of life, birth, death and rebirth until we attain the Nirvana." So, it is fitting that this last film should have been the storyteller making a film in India.

The pivotal sexual awakening scene with the female protagonist, Adela, played by Judy Davis, fascinated David. He had been to Khajuraho many times and was mesmerized by the temples there covered with erotic friezes; now, at last, in this scene, he had an opportunity to use them. They never ceased to excite him and I have so many photographs of these sensual figures in every sexual position.

He visited the temples at different times during the day so that he would capture the figures in different lights.

Then there were locations he wished to use – the blasting of holes through the rocks of "eternal" India for the scene of the caves, for instance – that got him into all sorts of difficulties with the Indian people. Of course, journalists blew this out of all proportion and David was described as the Englishman who desecrated the Indian landscape. Eddie Fowlie, his best friend and "scout", together with Kathleen, his wife found most of the locations and as usual made all the miracles happen. I watched him at work when he did the recces for *Nostromo* in Mexico and he really was miraculous, a sort of mixture of Long John Silver and a boy scout. He was David's second set of eyes.

There was, however, one member of the "family" missing; David yearned for his art director, John Box, who encapsulated his vision and turned it into reality. They had fallen out during the "trials" of *Bounty*, in Tahiti. John Brabourne finally made contact with him and without much ado, or maybe just a little, they agreed that their long friendship should override such grievances. John wrote a rather touching letter to David saying "I ask for your forgiveness for my wretched behaviour in Bora Bora. It has given me untold shame and misery."

Freddie Young, the oldest member of the "family", older than David, did not come on board and his operator, Ernie Day, was hired as cinematographer. And last, but certainly not least, David's right arm, Maggie Unsworth, his faithful continuity lady, joined him.

For David, it was an uphill battle all the way with actors, the cameraman and the production team; he should have been exhausted and would have been had he been bored, but here he was a man of seventy-plus making a movie again, doing what he most loved. The adrenalin drove him. At the start of the film he said, **"I was like an engine that needed running in again"** – he then became the bull

Dame Peggy Ashcroft
(OPPOSITE), **James Fox**
(ABOVE LEFT) **and Victor**
Bannerjee (ABOVE RIGHT)
interpret Forster's/Lean's
insight into India.

ABOVE CENTRE: **Poster**
for *Gandhi*.

that charged after the bandalleros had been lodged. He had promised editing credit to Eunice Mountjoy but back in England he simply said, "Directed and Edited by me – I'm going to take editing credit on this." Perhaps the greatest recognition of credit where credit is due came from Margaret Thatcher when she proposed him for a knighthood, which was announced in June 1984.

The premieres of *A Passage to India* took place in America in December of that year. David refused to attend the New York premiere because of the memory of that evening at the Algonquin Hotel when the critics had slated him a decade and a half before. This remained an ever-open wound. Ironically, the tide had turned. Since then, Richard Schickel had become film critic for *Time* magazine and now David was honoured with the cover, a great achievement for any director. David once asked me if I believed in "come uppance", which I firmly do and Richard Schickel certainly got his as he agonized over the article. I suppose he made his apology when he wrote "For a man like him, austere and passionate, to attempt a comeback after these misadventures and at his age was an act of extraordinary creative nerve."

A Passage to India received eleven Academy Award nominations, including Best Director and Best Screenplay for David. *Amadeus* ran way with everything that year but *Passage* won two, Best Supporting Actress, which went to Peggy Ashcroft for the part of Mrs Moore, and Best Music Score Score, which went to Maurice Jarre. However, my own opinion is, thank God he made the film and thank God he got the credits BUT all those wasted years nursing a grievance when he should have said to himself and the public "I'll show you – you ain't seen nothin' yet."

From India we jump to Spain, some three years later. David was working on the script of *Nostromo* when the telephone rang and Anne Coates announced to David that Columbia and a film preservationist, Bob Harris, were going to restore *Lawrence of Arabia*. The look on his face was memorable and when he replaced the receiver, he didn't say a word. He got up, walked over to me and threw his arms around me exclaiming "I'm so proud. Isn't it wonderful of them." He wanted to be involved to do a "fine cut" on the film, as there had not been enough time back in 1962 to do this. Bob said when he commenced the work, "I had begun the restoration of *Lawrence of Arabia* because I wanted to see it complete and in proper form. I had always felt that it was the finest film ever made – the pinnacle of motion picture art. It was the most expensive, extensive and difficult film ever restored."

In fact, it was Bob who had originally suggested the idea of restoring *Lawrence* to Columbia and David Puttnam, then President, agreed. Material was shipped from around the world. Problems occurred, Columbia reneged on the deal made with Bob and at the last minute threw in a killer deal point and the project headed towards litigation. David Puttnam tried to move it forward but not before he started running into his own problems at Columbia. Dawn Steel became president and Martin Scorsese appealed to her to sort out the litigation problem. Dawn did not know about the lawsuit and said to Marty "Are we suing someone or is someone suing us?" Marty laughed, "You better get into this. The original negative from 1962 is corroding." That did it and she did it.

It had grossed a lot of money for the studios. Twenty minutes had been cut from the original. There were two separate cuts and David insisted that Sam Spiegel, the producer of the film had cut the picture without his knowledge. Many of his colleagues disagree. One can go on endlessly about this but I can only say what I think happened.

David had a retentive memory, I don't think one can doubt that and he certainly would not have forgotten a "cut" such as this but I think what can be said is that there was a misunderstanding and that David's interpretation was misconstrued. Yes, he did agree to cut a few minutes out because he felt that the length of the film should have been slightly shorter and carefully trimmed but, what he claimed he did not agree to and did not know about, was that Sam went back and cut out more. So, when he referred to "the rats" having been at the negative, it was the second cut made by Sam that he was referring to. He would have to have been almost "gaga" to have removed footage to benefit the film then, twenty-seven years later, to replace that same footage. How would he have explained that! Moreover, who the hell cares who cut what; at least now, thanks to Dawn Steel, Columbia, Bob Harris, Jim Painten and, most of all, Steven Spielberg and Martin Scorsese, we have the most beautifully restored masterpiece. Also let us not forget David who gave it the final "Director's Cut".

At the 1989 New York premiere of the reissue of *Lawrence of Arabia* David said:

I remember something, which was said to me on December 16, 1962 after the New York premiere of *Lawrence*. After the screening, David O Selznick took my arm and we walked in silence on Fifth Avenue. Suddenly, he stopped, faced me and said, "David, listen to me: When *Gone with the Wind* was released everyone said to me, 'It's too long. You must cut the film' and I resisted. Your film is wonderful. They will tell you exactly the same: 'It's too long.' But I'm going to advise you to leave it alone, don't cut it. Well, it's taken me twenty-seven years! I suppose you can say, I followed his advice.

MY DEAR RICHARD,

SANDY AND I HAVE JUST FLOWN BACK TO THE TAJ IN DELHI
BECAUSE THE SRINAGAR COMMUNICATIONS ARE UNRELIABLE,
THE HOTEL IS TERRIBLE, WE ALL HAD FLU AND SOMEONE BROKE
MY TYPEWRITER.

YOUR MATTER OF FACT HBO — CHICKEN AND EGG LETTER
PUTTING US BACK TO SQUARE ONE JUST ABOUT PUT THE LID
ON IT. I DID NOT REPLY TO YOUR CABLES BECAUSE WE
ARE OBVIOUSLY IN NO POSITION TO SAY ANYTHING TO ERNIE AND
THE GOOD NEWS ABOUT KATE BECOMES GALLOWS
HUMOUR.

ANYHOW, THE KASHMIR LOCATION IS AN ADMIRABLE CONTRAST
TO CHANDRAPORE, EDDIE AND KATHLEEN ARE DRIVING THE CAR
BACK NEXT WEEKEND, MY TYPEWRITER AND I ARE BEING
REPAIRED AND I HOPE TO START THE REWRITE TOMORROW.

LOVE FROM US BOTH,

DAVID.

OPPOSITE AND LEFT: *A Passage to India.*

ABOVE: Script notes from David's travels.

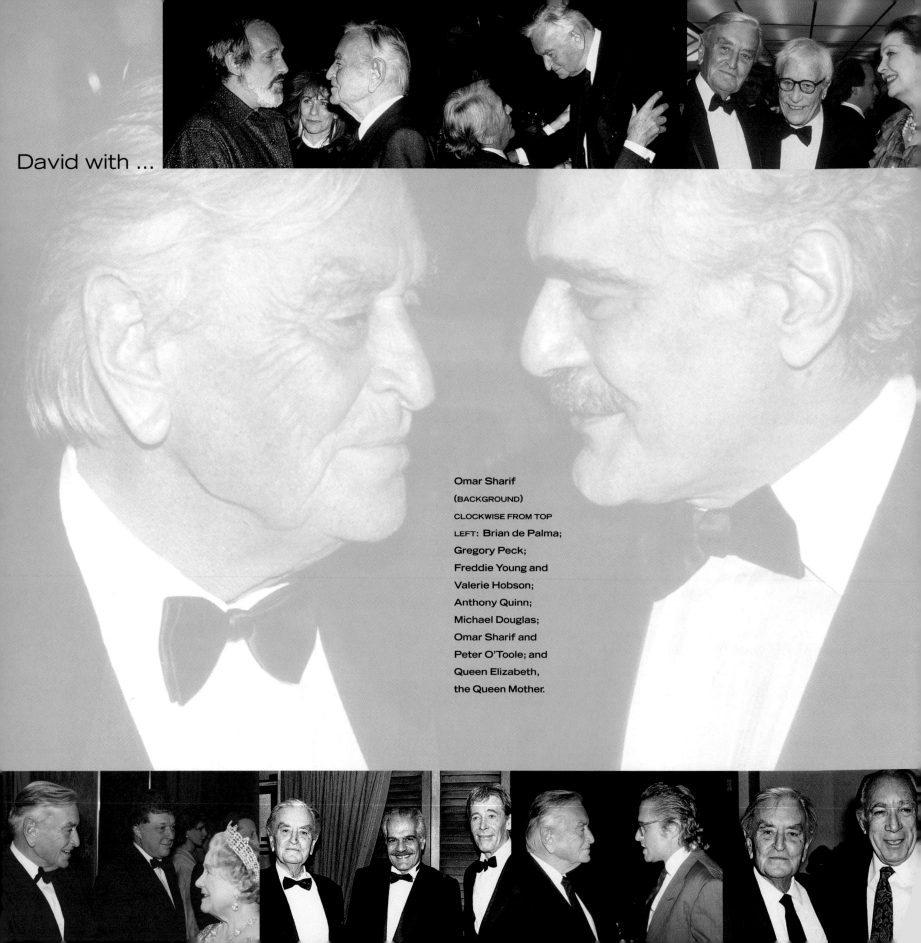

David with ...

Omar Sharif
(BACKGROUND)
CLOCKWISE FROM TOP
LEFT: Brian de Palma;
Gregory Peck;
Freddie Young and
Valerie Hobson;
Anthony Quinn;
Michael Douglas;
Omar Sharif and
Peter O'Toole; and
Queen Elizabeth,
the Queen Mother.

There are the few who ask, "Did David exaggerate what was necessary for his own purposes?" Adrian Turner, a film journalist and author of several film biographies, including *The Making of Lawrence of Arabia*, says that David only agreed to the restoration of *Lawrence* because he wanted the money for *Nostromo*. At that time, I can truthfully say that the financial structure for the film was already in place and David did not need to advertise *Lawrence* nor himself as a director. *Lawrence*, David and the rest of his films had already stood the test of time. Apart from this, any director would be proud that a film that he or she had directed twenty-seven years before was being released again. Adrian had approached David because he wanted to write a biography but David refused to co-operate so I think Mr. Turner's remarks may perhaps be tainted with "sour grapes".

David worked in the cutting room with Anne Coates, Bob and Jim. Bob was in awe of David, which made him very nervous but David noticed his nervousness and made a conscious effort to make him feel more comfortable. He admired Bob's expert editing and it became a very happy unit. David would arrive at the MGM lot early in the morning and work right through the day with a short break for lunch. He enjoyed being back in the cutting room. I remember several evenings where Bob's eyes had practically sunk into the back of his head and it was about ten thirty. "Let's go and eat," Bob said. "Are you tired?" said the eighty-year-old David, "let's go on another half an hour." Slowly, Bob began to relax and they finally became great friends.

"The Americans have been wonderful to me," David said. "They really love movies and respect movie-makers and the great thing about them is that they love success whereas the British hate you for succeeding."

During the publicity tours and premieres, which he made for the release of the film in New York, Washington and Los Angeles, I witnessed how good they were to him and what respect they had for him. He was treated like a God, and his talent was praised to such an extent that I became acutely aware of his embarrassment and his shyness. At the same time, I knew he was deeply touched and emotional. The film received wonderful reviews in the press and after he had sat through the film again some twenty-seven years after making it he said: "It looks bloody good, you know. I know I was there but it doesn't feel that it has very much to do with me. I could almost anticipate the dialogue but I feel tremendously removed from it."

Illness prevented him from going to the European premieres but he was anxious that I should attend the London premiere. We managed to get him to record a speech, which preceded the film. It was so sad that he could not be there to see how well it was received; it was also sad that he could not be at the one premiere that to him was "home". I rushed to the hospital directly afterwards forcing a smile on my face to describe every little detail but it was with a heavy heart that I did this. I felt very alone there in the Odeon cinema imagining his absent reaction. It would have been memorable for me to have shared his enthusiasm.

But, the warrior was to rise again from battle as the American Film Institute awarded him with the greatest honour that a director can receive: The Lifetime Achievement Award, which is presented annually to a " … recipient … whose talent has in a fundamental way advanced the film art; whose accomplishment has been acknowledged by scholars, critics, professional peers and the general public; and whose work has stood the test of time."

The award is usually given to an American (with the exception of another British great, Alfred Hitchcock) and past recipients have included James Stewart, Jack Lemmon and Fred Astaire. But as Gregory Peck, who hosted the ceremony on March 8, 1990, and was another recipient of the award, said, "Sometimes you just have to bend the rules." So, it was "A Salute to Sir David Lean".

A dinner was given in his honour which about two thousand people attended and there were tributes from his friends and peers including, Billy Wilder, John Mills, James Fox, Steven Spielberg, Angelica Houston and Martin Scorsese.

Everyone was waiting for David's speech. Perhaps he went a little too far in denouncing "the money men," producers and studio heads, when he told them that "they could afford to lose some" but he meant well and simply wanted them to recognize young talent.

"Give young directors a chance, take risks and put some money their way. It's a tough job being a director. One needs luck. Anyway, I wish them luck".

After his speech there was a standing ovation. When the applause finally stopped, Jack Lemmon said "goodnight" like this:

A friend of David's recently said, "One of the mistakes people make nowadays is thinking that a film unit is a democracy. It's not. It's a kingdom and everyone nurtures the wishes of the king." Well, with that in mind, let us not say goodnight, let's just simply say, "Long Live the King."

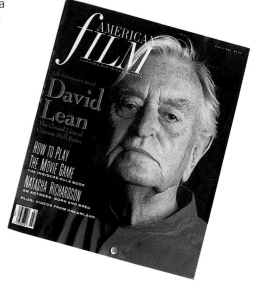

16   INSURANCE

I don't know of one director who doesn't go down on one knee whenever
The Bridge on the River Kwai or *Lawrence of Arabia* is discussed.

STEVEN SPIELBERG

AS I TAP AWAY AT MY COMPUTER working on the last two chapters of this book and the last chapter of David's life, it suddenly occurs to me that I am sitting in the same chair, at the very same desk and facing the same view as David when he worked on the last few scenes of his adaptation of Joseph Conrad's *Nostromo*. The view is through the silver leaves of the olive trees to the Alpes Maritimes beyond; I hope that I will be encouraged to have the same inspiration as he did from this wonderful old olive mill. David finally finished the shooting script in January 1991. Filming was to commence in May of the same year but it never happened …

Let me take you back a few years to 1985 when we visited French Polynesia. This was to be David's last journey to his favourite corner of the world.

He was working on an adaptation of J.G. Ballard's *Empire of the Sun* when one day in Bora Bora he turned rather dramatically in his chair to face me, paused, took off his glasses, and those piercing eyes bore into mine. I waited through the "Lean" silence and knew if I waited long enough, thoughts would turn into words. Finally, they arrived and he announced that he was not going to continue working on *Empire*. "Why?" I asked. "Because there is no dramatic arc and it's just a sort of diary of events." When David uttered such words I knew that he had

been agonizing over this decision for some time. This was final; no more conversation; it had become the love affair that was over.

Later that year, on our way home to London, we visited Hong Kong and crossed to China. Shanghai was on our itinerary as we wanted to sail to the mouth of the Yangtse river. At the same time we did a recce for *Empire of the Sun* as the film was originally going to be shot there. We stayed at the best hotel, The Peace. David was by this time in his life used to comfort; however, it seemed as if nothing had been done to The Peace since World War Two. As usual, round about seven o'clock in the evening David decided to take a bath. The carpet was heavily stained and filthy so David was naked apart from a pair of slippers. He popped his head round the bathroom door and announced that there was no plug for the bath. Quickly, I devised a plug out of an ashtray and a plastic bag and the tub was promptly filled. I heard nothing more until there was a shout from the bathroom. He did not need to explain as by this time the water was seeping into the bedroom. "What has happened to the plumbing?" he enquired. "There is none," was my answer. I'm sure if shooting had taken place there; a new hotel would have been built. I thought to myself at the time that all hell would have let loose and I was pleased that he had decided against the project.

Back to Bora Bora! The next day he started to read *Nostromo* which

LOCATION.

FAR LEFT: The inspirational desk.

CENTRE: David in Hong Kong en-route to Shanghai.

LEFT: David's meticulous notes on an adaptation of *Empire of the Sun*.

RIGHT: John Box's recce notes for *Nostromo*.

OPPOSITE: Christopher Hampton, who worked with David on the script of *Nostromo*.

THIS TOWER WILL EVENTUALLY BECOME THE LIGHTHOUSE

HOUSE IN THIS AREA

GENERAL LAYOUT.

CAN CHANGE SHAPE OF THE TOWER

HOUSE

GENERAL LAYOUT - FACING SOUTH [BEACHES

ACCESS ROAD

HOUSE IN THIS AREA

P.O.V FROM BOTTOM OF LIGHTHOUSE TOWARDS HOUSE.

P.O.V FROM HOUSE TOWARDS TOWER LIGHTHOUSE

FACING SOUTH

THIS SITE IS LESS THAN 10 MINUTES FROM THE HARBOUR SITE PAGE "A"

ALTERNATIVE P.O.V FROM HOUSE

P.O.V FROM HOUSE DOWN TO BEACH.
You can have as much Beach as you want
or as little as you want – The hatched
area indicates how we could reduce the
beach or you may decide you only want
Small Beach 1 which can be increased
in size. This is the beach next to the
big hole – There are several alternative
"ways-down".

he had tried to read before he had never made it beyond the first two hundred and fifty pages. "He never seems to get to the plot, the story, the once upon a time."

Maggie Unsworth and Robert Bolt had tried and tried to get him to read the book for years as both thought it could be a great Lean movie but David had never shown any enthusiasm. Now, however, I noticed that he had not picked up his camera for two days and he was immersed in the book. I did not ask him a single question; I knew that he would talk about it when he was ready. Finally, he said, "You know although this all takes place at the end of the nineteenth century and into the twentieth, it's so modern – all about corruption, greed and power, the disease of today! Wonderful characters." That did it; his engine was fired, he was excited, fearful and dry-mouthed. This was the beginning of the new love affair. The blueprint started to form in his head. Back in London, he started work on the script with Christopher Hampton, who was recommended to him by Maggie.

Christopher had worked mostly for theatre. His work included *The Philanthropist* and adaptations from Ibsen and Molière. He was later to write the screenplay for *Dangerous Liaisons*, from his theatrical adaptation of Pierre Choderlos de Laclos's *Les Liasons Dangereuses*, and *Carrington* which he also directed. He already knew *Nostromo* as he had prepared a synopsis for television, a version in seven one-hour episodes. Christopher was on board and that made David relax to a degree. The mouth became a little less dry and the fear a little less as he now had a "word man".

Christopher would arrive at Narrow Street each morning and the two would work through the morning until lunchtime. I used to be summoned to bring pots of espresso coffee during this time, possibly to boost David's low blood pressure. Lunch would be ready at one-thirty precisely. Unlike Robert, who was used to working with David, Christopher came face-to-face with David's insecurities. This was difficult. On first meeting, David appeared aloof. In fact, this apparent aloofness covered an immense shyness. Behind closed doors, off-stage, there would be a display of temper because David was more nervous than the actor who was downstairs in his study waiting for an interview. Christopher coped well but sometimes it used to get to him.

I did the cooking with my "sous chef" Fred. I would listen to the lift ascending from the study and Fred and I awaited the mood that would soon be upon us.

If we heard laughter, we breathed a sigh of relief. If we heard no sound at all then their footsteps would tell us all. Often, Christopher would appear in the kitchen

MARINA

Vivienda
Cochiqueras
Horno
INT. GRAN SALA
STREET
GARDEN
Estanque
Alta
EXT. INTENDENCIA
INT. INTE
INT-EXT
NEWSPAPER OFFICE
40 SECONDS
30 SECONDS
GOULD'S PATIO
STREET
PLAZA

33
28
27
19
20

Telefónica

ROAD

TO MOJACAR PARADOR 5 MINS.

TO SULACO
HARBOUR
12 MINS
LIGHTHOUSE 15 MINS

Mojacar

HARBOUR
OF SULACO   (GOLFO PLACIDO)

WAY TO
OPEN SEA

IS NOT FAR FROM TORRELAGUNA. IN SUMMER THE
GROUND IS FULL OF TALL WAVING GOLDEN GRASS
5 HIGH.   DOWN BY THE WATER IS A SMALL TOWN

Sir David Lean
Sun Wharf
Narrow Street
Limehouse
London
E14 8DQ
INGLETERRE

PHOTOS
FOTOS
N.C.V.

The many aspects
in the development of
a movie – *Nostromo*.

JUST AROUND THIS CORNER WILL BE

I THINK WE CAN CREATE AN
EXCELLENT GOULD GARDEN
AROUND THIS BOUGAINVILLEA

ahead of David. Sometimes, he would lift his head and say, "he's gone back to page one!" Need I say that lunch at times like this would be hell. Conversation would be sparse. David did not drink alcohol during the day and frowned on those who did, but poor Christopher needed it from time to time and I would notice a look of discontent on David's face when wine was offered.

Eddie Fowlie and John Box had recommended that David should recce Baja California, so we set off while Christopher remained in London to write.

David and I were away for six weeks. When we returned, David read Christopher's work and then began another year of rewriting. This was the last straw for Christopher who thought he was near the end of the screenplay. He had put all other work on hold, which included the screenplay of *Dangerous Liaisons*. Finally, he had to let go. David's perfectionism had got the better of him but they remained friends and had the utmost respect for one another.

As you will have gathered, David was not interested in the financing of film. His only interest was that there was enough in the budget to make the film he visualized. He mistrusted producers. However, he found Steven Spielberg acceptable as a producer. They respected one another. Steven wore the hat of producer/director so they both talked the same language. "I don't know of one director who doesn't go down on one knee whenever *The Bridge on the River Kwai* or *Lawrence of Arabia* is discussed," says Spielberg. "I have a great deal of reverence for David. He has a much broader movie vocabulary than a lot of directors, including myself. **He's the last of a generation of classical artists as picture makers.**"

Steven had been going to produce *Empire* but when he heard that David had fallen out of love with the subject, he asked David if he minded if he made the film. David did not object and told Steven about his ideas for *Nostromo*. "As far as I'm concerned," he said, "you can direct the Yellow Pages," so much admiration had he for David's films. He trusted David and was willing to produce *Nostromo*.

Steven was to direct *Empire of the Sun*; David was to direct *Nostromo*; Steven would take both films to Warner Bros. where Terry Semel was head of studio and raise US$30 million for each film. It all sounded perfect and David was hard at work with the script. However, nothing goes smoothly in the film industry and this is where things began to unravel. David was summoned to Los Angeles to see Terry Semel. On

LEFT: An *American Film* article on *Nostromo*.

RIGHT: The "Master Builder" on his recce in Mexico.

MARLON BRANDO

10 April 1989

Mr. David Lean
Sun Wharf No.30
Narrow Street
London E14 8DQ
England

Dear David:

As the elephant is slow to mate I too find myself irritatingly reluctant to make swift decisions in respect to scripts. At the first reading of the script of "Nostromo", my reaction was unreservedly enthusiastic. At the second reading two weeks later, I was even more impressed with what I assume to be your collaboration with Robert Bolt in the creation of the story. There are simply no scenarios that I have read in recent times that leave me with any enthusiasm whatsoever. The happy exception is "Nostromo ."

Most film makers today are only interested in financial successes. One has never had that feeling in any of of your works that you have ever had one eye cocked on the pound and to the surprise of many, I am sure including yourself, a good number of your films have had extraordinary financial rewards. You are the last of a breed, David. I don't want to sound maundlin in my praise, but I was simply delighted with the story. Its comment on the passing parade was trenchant without being heavy handed, biting without being bitter and one heard the sock of the arrow as it met the mark.

And now on to grizzly matters. I have t
one of which is a film to be done in Can
The other matter pertains to a script tha
The financiers have advanced me a mill

Casting the net.
LEFT: A letter from Marlon Brando to David discussing his possible involvement in *Nostromo*.

BOTTOM, LEFT TO RIGHT: Christophe Lambert; Paul Scofield; and Isabella Rosselini.

OPPOSITE TOP LEFT: David with Serge Silberman. RIGHT: David with Akira Kurosawa.

OPPOSITE, BOTTOM: Mike Medavoy.

arrival at the Bel Air hotel, I slowly realized that it was Steven he was to see the next day and not Terry Semel.

Perhaps Semel had chosen to leave decisions of the screenplay to Steven but David arrived back at the hotel in the evening absolutely humiliated. According to David, Steven had argued with him about the one part of the script that was the key to the whole story and characters and, if he changed it, David felt that the film would be a disaster. We never heard from Terry Semel and when we got back to London a telephone call announced that Steven and Warner Bros. had pulled out. I really do not know what happened behind closed doors with Steven and David but I know David was very hurt and that hurt was possibly displayed in anger. That's the way he was – ultra sensitive. Anyway, there he was without a producer. Where to go from here.

A film director may seem to some a rather glamorous profession. Once you win one or more Oscars, it is, but getting to that level is difficult and often painful. All responsibility falls on the shoulders of the director and discipline is of prime importance. David always described it as a lonely job. When writing a script, he was not at all sociable, explaining that he could not break the flow. I would try to persuade him to leave his typewriter for an hour or two and have dinner with friends but he resisted. **"Why don't you live with a nine to fiver!!"** he said. Often, we would have dinner in total silence with just the clink of metal on china until his chair would be pushed back crunching on the stone floor, the lift door would open and close and he would descend to his study to continue writing for the rest of the evening. Therefore, social gatherings were few and far between. I did understand, as he found writing difficult and had to form a complete blueprint in his head, which barely altered. Complete concentration was needed.

One invitation did, however, bring a smile to his face. We were invited to a dinner given in honour of the director, Akira Kurosawa. David greatly admired his films and accepted. I found myself sitting next to a great producer, Serge Silberman, who had produced all the later Buñuel and Kurosawa films. I learned that he greatly admired David and his parting words, before the evening ended, were, "Call me if there is anything I can ever do for David." I promised to do so.

David hardly ever made telephone calls. He would call people he was working with such as Robert, Maggie and Tony Reeves, his lawyer. Other than that, hardly ever.

Ideas for producers were going round and round in my head and I had told David about Serge. One day I said "Why don't you call him?" He refused but I had sown a seed. A few days later, he asked me to call

Serge and I pushed the telephone into his hand. Serge was wonderful and came over to London within twenty-four hours to have a meeting with David.

Here was a producer that David did not know so automatically the hackles rose. David was not only suspicious of any producer but Serge was a small man and David used to think that small men were always trying to prove themselves. "Babe, two feet tall – beware!" I thought this was rather unfair on Serge as he was being so helpful and felt he could arrange finance for the film. War, unfortunately, was declared between the two and I was pig in the middle, trying to achieve the impossible. What was needed was a line producer instead of me, but Serge would not hear of it. We had now moved into our house in the South of France and Robert Bolt and David were working together again. Maggie, Robert, Joyce Gallie (a casting director and now one of my closest friends), actors and actresses – all came and went.

By this time, Columbia Tristar and the BBC together with a syndicate organized by Serge were involved and the budget had reached US$48 million. At this stage, one would have expected a smooth run but there was an enormous clash of personalities between David and Serge. Both wanted creative control but David would not tolerate any interference from Serge. The thought of a producer being creative went against the grain. Clearly there were misunderstandings, some caused by a

LEFT AND ABOVE: David's recce shots for *Nostromo* – Cuba and Spain.

BELOW: Margaret Tiffin, a friend.

BELOW, CENTRE: Joyce Gallie, casting director on *Nostromo*.

BOTTOM: Sarah Foster, David's PA.

language barrier. It was therefore fortunate that I speak French, which enabled me to smooth over differences between the two. If I did not get there in time there would be an enormous eruption, followed by a three-day sulk and ending with a peace offering from Serge who would arrive bearing cool boxes full of David's favourite cheeses and chocolate truffles.

David was eighty-two and, to be fair to Serge, I am sure he found it quite difficult to persuade financiers to back him. David, on the other hand, used to shout that with his track record and never having lost the Studios one penny why shouldn't he have his own way. Secretly, David thought that this film could be bigger and better than *Lawrence* and he tried every way he could to persuade Serge to shoot the film in 65-mm negative. Serge would not hear of it. David wanted to cast George Corraface, an unknown film actor, to play *Nostromo*. George was recommended to David by Joyce Gallie and Peter Brook and would have been fantastic in the part. Serge would not hear of it. David wanted Isabella Rossellini and Irene Papas. Again, Serge put up an argument, and so it went on and on. Joyce was having a very difficult time with Serge, who just would not and could not listen. All this used to rub off on everyone involved and the two people who were left to cope with it were Sarah Foster, who had moved to France with us, and myself. I used to fall into bed exhausted, only to toss and turn trying to think of a way that I could make everyone agree. I suppose I felt some sympathy for Serge as he had to come up with big box office names to satisfy the studio; but he didn't know how to handle David. Instead of discussing suggestions when they were put to him, Serge opposed them immediately. David's reaction was to charge like a bull. It was frustrating for David and I, more than anyone, could see how it was affecting him. These interferences disturbed his creativity and my heart went out to him.

Doom and gloom. David would escape to the bath. Peace at last. He was alone with his thoughts. Often I would sit with him on the edge of the bath and he would go over ideas he had for the film. Outside the bathroom, everyone was frenetic as David had writer's block. Although he gave me full artistic control on the house design, he retained a director's veto on the subject of showers. He would have no showers in the house. Consequently any visiting health freak who "needed an invigorating shower" was despatched to the poolside shower. We were nearly at the end of week two of the block. Bathing time had become longer and longer and sometimes lunch would be delayed until he was ready which may have been some two hours later than the original time he had suggested. The mood became blacker. The problem was the

---

...with delicate fronds of...shoulders supported by a slope of coral draped in the barely recognisable remains of a suit with wisps of fabric streaming out in the current.

The SKULL is looking up at something:

A column of seaweed sways to a halt then starts to swing back.

Its ragged shadow moves across a shining SILVER INGOT half buried in the sand, embossed with the words 'SAN TOME'. On SOUND another rumble, quite close.

A BUBBLE of AIR, the size of a child's balloon has released itself from the seabed and is floating up through the water.

The SKULL is watching it. MUSIC begins.

The BUBBLE floats away, higher and higher, towards the great yellow disk of the SUN.

CLOSE on the SKULL, watching.

CUT.

2. EXTERIOR.   GOLFO PLACIDO.   DAY.

The BUBBLE bursts on the surface. The MUSIC builds.

LONG SHOT. Ripples spread out across a great stretch of still water reaching to the horizon, the GOLFO PLACIDO. The MUSIC rises to a climax.

A LONG SHOT in the opposite direction discloses that the landward side of the Gulf is dominated and enclosed by a great range of snow-capped mountains, the ANDES. Thousands of feet below the snow is a brilliantly green band of TROPICAL FOREST with ravines leading down to an area of scrub and cactus towards the small run-down town and harbour of SULACO dating from a couple of centuries ago.

3. EXTERIOR SULACO.   THE PLAZA MAYOR.   DAY.

LONG SHOT. We are looking down from high up through massive walls, stone figures and a cross onto the town square which is dominated by an EQUESTRIAN STATUE of King Carlos IV of Spain. Black flags figured with a dragon in ornamental gold fly in the hot air.

ABOVE: **The first page of Robert Bolt's script for *Nostromo*.**

first scene in *Nostromo*. He could not crack the problem of how to go from an underwater skeleton clasping a silver ingot and dressed in a shredded Edwardian frock coat, to a shot of the small South American port where the story is set. It was agonizing not only for him but the whole household who had been sucked into this problem. Suddenly, one day, the house rocked to a shrill cry from David. I rushed to the bathroom dreading what I would find. There was no pool of blood on the floor, no limp body in the bath. Instead, a triumphant David.

"I've got it."

"Got what?"

"It's so simple."

"As the skeleton rocks in the underwater current, an air bubble is released from deep within the body. The camera follows the rising bubble and travels with it until it breaks the surface. Rings of water caused by the released air bubble takes the eye to a small port which sets the scene for the story".

How he came to this decision, I will never know.

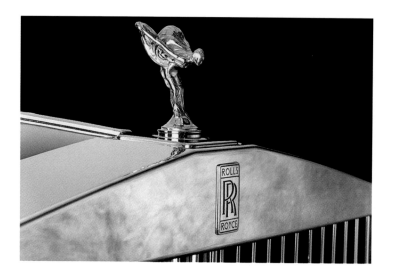

17 COMPLETION BOND

He was the most extraordinary man I ever knew.
LAWRENCE OF ARABIA

DAVID HAD NOT BEEN WELL, he had been suffering from 'flu and a doctor had put him on heavy doses of the steroid, cortisone. At that time I naively had total confidence in the medical profession, however, cortisone reduces the efficiency of the immune system, weakens the muscles, causes mood swings and must be reduced gradually. As a result of taking the drug David became excessively "rumpled, crumpled and disgruntled." He felt so tired, was working so hard, for such long hours and had a grim determination not to give in. Illness was an unknown experience to David and because he was unable to cope with sympathy I had to gently support him in an unobtrusive fashion. With great difficulty I attempted to be cheerful. I hoped that he was unaware of both my deception and my pain, I simply wanted to enable him to achieve his passion to make *Nostromo*. I was convinced that his burning ambition would enable him to overcome illness, I longed for him to be indestructible. I wanted peace to return to his life and for him to enjoy once again all the pleasures of the house and garden in France and to hear the chirping of the birds that he so much loved.

By this time, the completion guarantors had demanded that he have a stand-by director – "in case I keel," said David. This was the last straw. This was an intruder. To explain how he was going to direct a picture to some stand-by director was impossible for him.

I had to return to London as I had let my house and the tenants had done a great job in destroying it so I set about putting it back together again as quickly as I could in order to get back to David's side at the Moulin in France.

We talked three times a day and it was during one of these conversations that David paused and said **"Babe will you marry me?"** I then paused and, thinking he was teasing me, replied, **"You must be joking!"** (David was very sensitive about his marriages and we had never discussed marriage between us. It was enough just to be with him). The conversation continued, **"No, I'm not joking,"** he said. I was silent. By then, I knew he meant what he had said. I was silent because I was so touched and overcome with emotion. I said I would call him back. I was in the kitchen surrounded by builders and electricians, with wires hanging everywhere. The builders were Greek and bazooki

OPPOSITE: **The Rolls Royce "Spirit of Ecstacy", the constant woman in David's life.**

LEFT: **David on the terrace of Sun Wharf overlooking the Thames.**

FAR LEFT: "Babe will you marry me?": David and I at the Moulin.

LEFT: Wedding day: "Yes I do."

OPPOSITE: Me and my shadow – David with our cat, Groovy.

music filled the room. They turned to look at me and suddenly the room became silent. They downed tools and watched the tears streaming down my face. They couldn't understand what had happened until I told them not to worry; nothing terrible had happened but something wonderful had. They immediately went out to buy a bottle of champagne while I called David and uttered only one word, **"Yes."**

I returned to the Moulin to find David and Sarah, his PA, plotting and planning our wedding. It was such a beautiful moment in my life marred only by David not being in the best of health. I could think of nothing else other than getting him well for his latest reel obsession, *Nostromo*, and getting it a green light.

During this time David's dry sense of humour was at its height; his health began to take a turn for the better and we seemed to be nearing the end of all the trials of getting this film on to the screen. The Moulin was like a hotel, "hot bedding," David said. Nevertheless, he so enjoyed the "to-ing and fro-ing" of people and the hilarious dinners round the table with Mike Medavoy, and Jonathan Darby from Tri-Star, who frequently came over from Los Angeles. But, with the wedding and the film coinciding, the telephone never stopped and this really got on his nerves.

One evening, when it must have been about the tenth call, albeit usually something to do with the film, a wicked grin appeared on David's face. He looked at me and said. "Don't answer the telephone – give it to me." I did and of course it promptly rang again. He answered and I only heard two words, "F--k off." I laughed. "What's so funny" he said, knowing well what had amused me. These words sounded so strange coming from this most elegant man. "You've missed your vocation," I said. "You would have made a wonderful actor." We did learn later that the call he had answered so succinctly was from the studio in Los Angeles.

The date of the wedding – December 14 – loomed and Sarah had organized hotels near the house for the overseas guests. This was

difficult for her as the French have the habit of closing all hotels during the month of November and December but somehow she seemed to reopen them. Guests had started to arrive. The telephone never stopped; the rain was torrential; the roof started to leak since the builders had forgotten the insulation; action never stopped. David could not work and our wedding should not have interfered. **"After all, we're only getting married – what's all the fuss about?"** Three days before the day, it all got to him and as we sat down to have a drink together in the evening he said to me, "Babe, book a room at the Negresco and let's get out of here until we get married."

I was astonished and said I couldn't leave Sarah with all these arrangements. She did speak a little French but not enough and I thought I could not leave her to cope on her own. "OK," he said. "If you are not coming with me, I'm going alone." David alone – whoops!!! I arranged for André, who looked after us at the Moulin, to go with him and off they went. I may as well have gone with him as he called the next morning to say that the food was inedible so I gathered my market basket and made the trip to Nice every day with goodies. I know it was a game he played in order to get me there. Guests had started to arrive from abroad.

We were not completely organized but that did not matter, we still had a little more time ahead of us. I remember collapsing on the floor with a glass of wine in my hand when the telephone rang. David had decided he wanted to come home for supper but be back at the hotel soon afterwards in order to continue working. Panic set in; menus were pushed together and all was ready. At the precise time of his warned arrival, the door opened and in he walked. We gasped. He was dressed in his pyjamas and dressing gown. Both, I am pleased to say were elegant garments but I could never get over the fact that he had walked through the foyer of the Negresco dressed for bed and moreover did not care. He certainly could carry it off and had. We fell about laughing.

He enjoyed this scene and had done it on purpose to see our reaction.

We had a beautiful wedding with so many of his friends and colleagues around him and Sarah had organized it all. We had the the idea of getting someone to drive "Babe", his claret-coloured friend, to France as we thought this would really cheer him up. This was truly one of the great things Sarah and I did and I will never forget David's face when he saw her parked outside the Moulin and we drove to the Town Hall in Mouans Sartoux to be married. We spent Christmas at home quite quietly as he was still working on the script. The monies were in place and the "master builder" John Box had designed the set. David had been going to shoot the studio work in Spain but he suddenly decided that the Victorine Studios in Nice had more appeal since he would be able to drive there each day and return to the Moulin in the evening. Another reason was that his hero, Rex Ingram, the director, had made pictures there in the 1920s.

Serge behaved very well over this sudden decision as it took a lot of rearranging. The scene was set. In my own mind at the time, I thought that all this would make him strong enough to overcome anything.

However, around Boxing Day, I noticed that David was not eating enough and seemed to have difficulty swallowing and talking. That was an agonizing time for me. I talked to Peter Wheeler, David's doctor, and made the decision to fly home to London. A tumour was found in his throat and shortly afterwards, cancer was diagnosed with radiotherapy the advised treatment. I will never forget the night Peter came to the door of my home in London, where we were staying at that time, to tell me the results of the CAT-scan that David had undergone that afternoon. I just looked into Peter's eyes and I knew it all before he uttered a word. I began to cry and Peter, quite correctly, told me to pull myself together and we went upstairs to tell David. He was so brave and said, **"Well, now I know, I'm going to fight it."** I must say he

ABOVE: Congregation:
the "reel" family at St
Paul's, October 1991.

RIGHT: Omar and George
Corraface.

OPPOSITE: The "real" family.

did for a while. After six weeks of radiotherapy the tumour had disappeared but he was tired and Quaker to the end, he did not want to appear undignified. He had never been ill before – David Lean was never sick. He was humiliated and, I know, at the end, he willed himself to go. **This was his final escape from the drudgery of reality.** Films had been his escape. This time, however, we saw the true director's cut, the silence was forever, and on April 16, 1991, he just gave up and I lost him. Not only had I lost him but the world had also lost him.

My closest friend, Margaret, and the ever-faithful Sarah were so kind to me and that was comforting. David's friends were wonderful, especially Maggie Unsworth, who telephoned me twice daily. John Box missed David and we sat together reminiscing. John poured out his woes about the times in Tahiti on the *Bounty*. He still felt very guilty. I tried to comfort him and I know that David had forgiven him. But, looking back at those early days after he'd gone, I realize that half my body had gone too. I know he would not have approved and I could

hear him saying "pull yourself together" and I did try very hard. It was at this time that I really missed my parents. They were lonely moments.

The funeral was organized by Sarah and Margaret, as I am ashamed to say I could not cope with it. Conversations flashed through my head. "I never went to my mother's funeral – I was in the desert when this telegram arrived. I was shooting *Lawrence*. I simply could not return." Neither did he go to Edward's funeral. He could not cope with illness or death and the thought of both frightened him. As I sat in the car with my best friend at my side on the way to the funeral, visions of that lion's head and those piercing eyes kept appearing and disappearing. As I stepped out of the car I froze. All I remember was Peter O'Toole's outstretched hand and the kindness and softness of James Fox.

Afterwards, back at Sun Wharf we had a party that David himself would have enjoyed and I am sure he would have wanted us to enjoy. A pianist played all the Cole Porter music he adored. I watched the trusted family, the cast in his life and felt proud. Two days later I received a letter from Alec Guinness, which simply said, "I owe my career to him."

Sarah and I returned to the Moulin. It was so hard as he was everywhere. I know Sarah would open cupboards and keep throwing things in the dustbin to make life easier for me. The warmth and the atmosphere helped me and I started to feel better. I thought of him way back in his life when he had a small allotment and was suffering a depression. He said putting his hands in the earth and creating growth made him well again. I did just that and finished working on the garden we had planned. I watched his beloved sunflowers and canna lilies bloom and tasted the muscatel grapes that we had planted together.

At the same time Sarah and I thought of his last send off – the memorial service. Suddenly, we thought of one of the first scenes in *Lawrence* – T.E. Lawrence's own memorial service at St Paul's Cathedral. I started to laugh as I could imagine David saying **"Too grand, my dear. Do I really deserve a place in there?"** The Dean could not have been nicer. He would be delighted. He took Sarah and me into the Cathedral and blessed us. After that the production started and it took us three months to plan the service. John Birt, Director General of the BBC, really orchestrated the nuts and bolts as I came up with the suggestions. There were a few hiccups but mostly everyone we wanted to participate, accepted.

Maurice had prepared a special arrangement of the film music with the Royal Philharmonic orchestra. He arrived from Los Angeles the day before the service. At the rehearsal that day, he discovered that there was a fifty-second echo within the Cathedral. It was a tense moment, Maurice was horrified. In the end, he just went with it and his overture to *Lawrence* was breathtaking.

And so to October 3, 1991, St Paul's Cathedral: filled with two thousand people, many whom David had personally known and many who had worked with him. If there was one aspect of his life and work that emerged from that day it was this: David's work was a demanding lover and friend, his absorption and obsession. At St Paul's his friends and colleagues lovingly shared their recollections of David's life, talent and spirit. This was a memorial to celebrate David, the film-maker and David, the man.

I was proud and deeply touched by those who spoke: Omar, reading the opening pages of *The Seven Pillars of Wisdom,* which had formed the basis for *Lawrence of Arabia*; John Mills reading from *Great Expectations*; Peter O'Toole's magnificent voice resounding throughout the vast space of the cathedral; Sarah Miles reading David's favourite speech from *In Which we Serve*, originally spoken by Celia Johnson; and the unknown actor, George Corraface, reading one of his speeches from *Nostromo*, David's unfinished requiem. Perhaps the most touching moment was when Robert Bolt slowly walked up to the rostrum, looked up and spoke four words: "He was my friend."

David had a dream and a vision, which he fulfilled for the rest of the world if not totally for himself. In genius, there is no boundary.

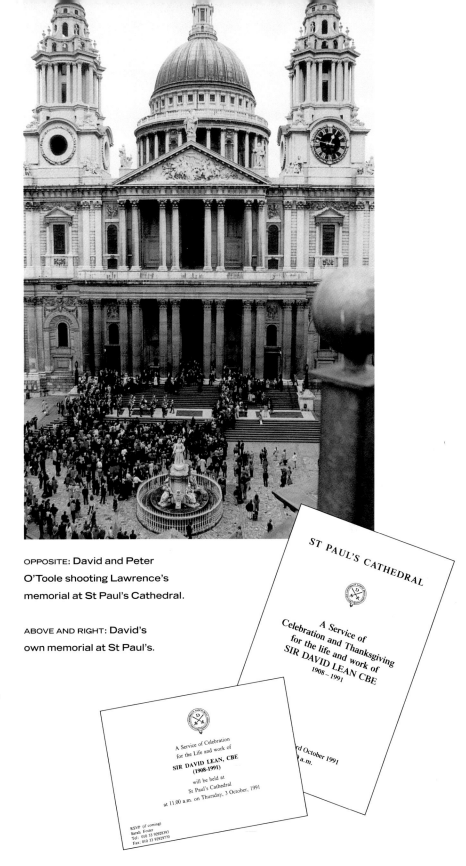

OPPOSITE: **David and Peter O'Toole shooting Lawrence's memorial at St Paul's Cathedral.**

ABOVE AND RIGHT: **David's own memorial at St Paul's.**

ST PAUL'S CATHEDRAL

A Service of Celebration and Thanksgiving for the life and work of SIR DAVID LEAN CBE 1908–1991

A Service of Celebration for the Life and work of **SIR DAVID LEAN, CBE (1908-1991)** will be held at St Paul's Cathedral at 11.00 a.m. on Thursday, 3 October, 1991

RSVP (if coming)
Sarah Foster
Tel: 010 33 92928393
Fax: 010 33 92929770

ABOVE: David's son Peter, Maggie Unsworth,
David Tringham and Hugh Hudson hold
David's Awards at the memorial.

BELOW: Ten years after: Steven Spielberg
and I accepting the Producers'
Guild of America Hall of Fame award
for *Lawrence of Arabia* 2001.

RIGHT AND ABOVE RIGHT:
The keepers of David's ashes.

The photograph of the sunflowers opposite was
David's last. I found the film in his camera some
months after he died. His great passion for this
flower captures all that he loved about people and
life, its open face, its hugeness, its ability to turn
towards the sun as he did. These thoughts are
symbolized in a shot he used in *Doctor Zhivago*.
As Lara departs from the love of her life Yuri, the
camera poignantly focuses on a large vase of dying
sunflowers shedding their petals.

I'm not a Quaker now. I don't know what I am. I
don't think, as Mrs Moore says, that it's a
Godless universe. But, I wouldn't know what
God is. We're still trying to find out what makes
us tick, like plumbers trying to mend
Swiss watches.

DAVID LEAN

I believe your name will be a household word.

GENERAL ALLENBY TO LAWRENCE IN *LAWRENCE OF ARABIA*.

INDEX

ACKNOWLEDGEMENTS

So many people who have contributed in helping to create this book. There would be added pages if all were to be named so I would like to take this opportunity to thank them for their encouragement and tireless labours.

However I feel I would like to personally thank but a few for their extraordinary efforts; John Spirit who spent many hours co-ordinating the text.

Lucy Lean-Rachou who helped enormously in the strategy of the book.

Thanks to those of you who have already researched David's work and have published their own books. However I am enormously grateful in this respect to Kevin Brownlow, Robert Morris and Lawrence Raskin and Stephen Silverman for treading the path before therefore making this book more comprehensive.

A warm embrace and sincere thanks for their kind permission to reproduce photographs: Richard Blanshard, Anthony Reeves, Mike Ross, Mike Tighe, Laura Tokeley, Mike Stevenson, David Tringham, Sir Anthony and Lady Havelock-Allan, John Box, David Bailey, Jill Kennington, Lord Snowdon, Issey Miyake, Fritz von der Schulenberg, Daniel Mennassian, Francois and Danielle Roux, Maurice Jarre, Tim Garland-Jones, Joan Cherrill, Ian Gordon for his help in editing, Sony Corporation, Fritz Friedman, Producers Guild of America, Doris Fowlie, Les Hodgson, Vic Simpson, Phil Hobbs, Dick Best, Ron Paquet, Leon Morgan, Tim Unsworth, Petra Bachstein, all at the British Film Institute and the American Film Institute.

I am so grateful to Omar Sharif for writing the foreword to this book which could not have happened without the help of Steve Kennis.

To our design team: many thanks to Penny Sutton who spent much time on design layouts and Arrow Offset Printers, design enactors.

Finally, I must mention people who have been closest to me whilst writing the book; first and foremost Barry Chattington, my housekeeper, Lucinda Silvestre, Red, my Burmese cat and last, but certainly not least, my close friend, Peter Lukas.

AND of course to David who gave me so much happiness and inspired me to write.

PICTURE CREDITS

All of the pictures included in this book are either original images by David Lean or owned by The David Lean Collection excepting those listed below. The authors would like to thank the following for their kind permission to reproduce these pictures in the book:

AKG 183; *Amateur Photographer* 14 (by kind permission of the publishers); *American Film Magazine* 211; AMPAS 16, 20, 25, 34–35, 36, 40, 42, 48, 50–51, 60 (x2), 70, 91, 104–5, 106, 107, 117, 118 (x2), 120, 122, 123, 125, 127, 137, 140–1, 152–3, 156–7, 164, 174; Andreas Von Einsiedel 160 (Condé Nast Publications Limited); Anthony Havelock-Allen 37; Aquarius 16, 154 (x2), 169; Archive NYC 23, 36, 52; Barry Chattington 18; British Film Institute 17 (x2), 20, 20–21, 22, 29, 36, 37, 45, 62, 69, 73, 106, 112–13, 130, 131, 132, 133, 137, 154, 154–5, 162, 162–3, 171 (x2), 177, 180, 182, 204, 205, 206, 207 (x2), 209 (x5); Christophe Lambert 222; Colombe d'Or 143; Columbia Tristar 58, 71, 116/117, 175, 176; Dalton Nicholson Collection 8, 47, 61, 76, 118, 135, 168, 175; David Bailey 179; David Tringham 92, 100; Doris Fowlie 94; Edward Scotland 2000 77; *Elle* 77; *Friend* (newspaper) 10; Horizon Pictures 98–99, 188; Hulton Getty 12, 19, 22 (x 3), 23 (x 4), 30, 31, 39, 41, 66-67, 69, 82, 109, 134, 187, 232; Isabella Rossellini 222; Jill Pennington 2–3, 227; Kevin Brownlow 32, 154, 180; KJD (Gary Leggett) 44 (x5.), 47, 61, 200, 207; Kobal Collection 49, 89, 105, 112, 118, 136, 202–3; Laurie's Hotel, Agra 193; Leighton Park School 14 (x 3); Leslie Hodgson 98–99; Lord Snowdon 121; M de Saurin 148, 149, 150, 151, 160–61; Magnum

Photos 52–53; Mary Evans Picture Library 13, 124; Maurice Jarre 177; MGM 110–11; Mike Medavoy 223; Mike Ross 31, 142, 144, 147, 226; Milepost 13; Mirror Syndication International 185; *Modern Wireless* 14 (by kind permission of the publishers); *Motion Picture* 14 (by kind permission of the publishers); Moviestore 125, 133, 217; *Nostromo* 20 (by kind permission of the Publishers); Penny Sutton 86, 144–5; Phil Hobbs 98-9; Photofest 24, 29, 38, 172, 184, 189; Picphotos 43, 68, 92; *Picturegoer* 14 (by kind permission of the publishers); Pinewood Studios 18; Producer's Guild (by kind permission of *USA Today*) 234; *Rainbow* (children's paper) 13; Rex Features 180, 223; Richard Blanshard 223; Robert Opie 15; Ronald Grant Archive 14, 16 (x2 pics.), 17, 18, 20 (x2 pics.), 37, 68, 90, 109, 128–9, 132, 170, 173, 184; Schulenburg 147 (The Interior Archive); Science Museum 169 (NMPFT/Science and Society Picture Library); Sidney Box Productions180; Technicolour 166; *Time* 200, 208; Timothy Unsworth 98-9; United Artists 134; University of Reading 181; Vera Campbell 13; Vic Simpson 95; Vintage Magazine Archive 13, 15.

The above credits are as accurate as the Authors can ascertain. Every effort has been made to acknowledge correctly and contact the source and/or copyright holder of each image and the authors apologise for any unintentional errors of omissions, which will be corrected in future editions of this book.